TECHNICAL REPORT

T0164183

Combat Support Execution Planning and Control

An Assessment of Initial Implementations in Air Force Exercises

Kristin F. Lynch, William A. Williams

Prepared for the United States Air Force

RAND PROJECT AIR FORCE

The research described in this report was sponsored by the United States Air Force under Contract F49642-01-C-0003. Further information may be obtained from the Strategic Planning Division, Directorate of Plans, Hq USAF.

Library of Congress Cataloging-in-Publication Data

Lynch, Kristin F.
    Combat support execution planning and control : an assessment of initial implementations in Air Force exercises / Kristin F. Lynch, William A. Williams.
        p. cm.
    Includes bibliographical references.
    ISBN 978-0-8330-3996-5 (pbk. : alk. paper)
    1. Command and control systems—United States. 2. United States. Air Force—Maneuvers. 3. Military planning—United States. I. Williams, William Appleman. II. Title.

UB212.L96 2009
358.4'133041—dc22

2009003509

The RAND Corporation is a nonprofit research organization providing objective analysis and effective solutions that address the challenges facing the public and private sectors around the world. RAND's publications do not necessarily reflect the opinions of its research clients and sponsors.

RAND® is a registered trademark.

Published 2009 by the RAND Corporation
1776 Main Street, P.O. Box 2138, Santa Monica, CA 90407-2138
1200 South Hayes Street, Arlington, VA 22202-5050
4570 Fifth Avenue, Suite 600, Pittsburgh, PA 15213-2665
RAND URL: http://www.rand.org/
To order RAND documents or to obtain additional information, contact
Distribution Services: Telephone: (310) 451-7002;
Fax: (310) 451-6915; Email: order@rand.org

Preface

Since 2000, RAND Project AIR FORCE (PAF) researchers have documented the need for a well-defined, closed-loop future ("TO-BE") combat support execution planning and control (CSC2) operational architecture that would enable the Air Force to achieve the goals of an air and space expeditionary force (AEF). Using lessons learned during Joint Task Force (JTF) Noble Anvil and Operation Enduring Freedom and an in-depth analysis of the processes associated with CSC2, PAF researchers defined a TO-BE operational architecture (Leftwich et al., 2002), which the Air Force is in the process of implementing. The CSC2 operational architecture calls for an integrated approach to providing service forces and sustaining them during joint combat operations. As the Air Force continues to enhance its expeditionary capabilities, exercises provide opportunities to evaluate the extent to which elements of the CSC2 architecture have been implemented, as well as areas that need additional improvements.

The research for this report was completed in 2004. While the agile combat support command and control system is continuing to evolve, a number of the findings in this report are still applicable.

This report presents an analysis of CSC2 implementation actions as observed during the Pacific Command (PACOM) exercise Terminal Fury 2004 (TF04) and the U.S. Air Forces in Europe (USAFE) exercise Austere Challenge 2004 (AC04). These operational-level command and control (C2) warfighter exercises presented an opportunity to compare the current ("AS-IS") CSC2 operational architecture, in two different theaters, with the Air Force future, or TO-BE, architecture.

While neither the PACOM nor the USAFE exercise was focused on combat support functional capability, each provided an operational environment in which combat support issues could be discussed and assessed. A joint PAF and Air Force assessment team, with Air Force strategic partners based in the continental United States (CONUS), reviewed the information flows and agile combat support (ACS) and operational processes and systems that linked combat support nodes with operational needs that were employed during these exercises. The team assessed the effectiveness of the CSC2 TO-BE nodes, information systems, and products available in a collaborative environment, as well as training and education. The assessments were not an evaluation of the exercise itself but an observation of some of the key CSC2 tasks, such as allocation of scarce resources, within an operational context of a major C2 exercise.

The Directorate of Logistics Readiness (HQ USAF/ILG) was assigned overall responsibility for the assessment. The Planning, Doctrine, and Wargames staff (HQ AF/ILGX) conducted the assessment in conjunction with RAND Corporation researchers, who worked in the Resource Management Program of Project AIR FORCE. The work was part of a project entitled "Balancing Combat Support Equipment Resources." The research for this report was completed in April 2004.

This report should be of interest to military commanders, logisticians, operators, civil engineers, C2 planners, and mobility planners throughout the Department of Defense, especially those in the Air Force and those who rely on Air Force bases and support to shape their combat capability.

This study is one of a series of RAND publications that address agile combat support issues in implementing the AEF. Other publications in the series include the following:

- *Supporting Expeditionary Aerospace Forces: An Integrated Strategic Agile Combat Support Planning Framework*, Robert S. Tripp, Lionel A. Galway, Paul S. Killingsworth, Eric Peltz, Timothy L. Ramey, and John G. Drew (MR-1056-AF). This report describes an integrated combat support planning framework that may be used to evaluate support options on a continuing basis, particularly as technology, force structure, and threats change.

- *Supporting Expeditionary Aerospace Forces: New Agile Combat Support Postures*, Lionel A. Galway, Robert S. Tripp, Timothy L. Ramey, and John G. Drew (MR-1075-AF). This report describes how alternative resourcing of forward operating locations can support employment time lines for future AEF operations. It finds that rapid employment for combat requires some prepositioning of resources at forward operating locations.

- *Supporting Expeditionary Aerospace Forces: A Concept for Evolving to the Agile Combat Support/Mobility System of the Future*, Robert S. Tripp, Lionel A. Galway, Timothy L. Ramey, Mahyar A. Amouzegar, and Eric Peltz (MR-1179-AF). This report describes the vision for the ACS system of the future based on individual commodity study results.

- *Supporting Expeditionary Aerospace Forces: Lessons From the Air War Over Serbia*, Amatzia Feinberg, Eric Peltz, James Leftwich, Robert S. Tripp, Mahyar A. Amouzegar, Russell Grunch, John G. Drew, Tom LaTourrette, and Charles Robert Roll, Jr. (MR-1263-AF, not available to the general public). This report describes how the Air Force's ad hoc implementation of many elements of an expeditionary ACS structure to support the air war over Serbia offered opportunities to assess how well these elements actually supported combat operations and what the results imply for the configuration of the Air Force ACS structure. The findings support the efficacy of the emerging expeditionary ACS structural framework and the associated but still-evolving Air Force support strategies.

- *Supporting Expeditionary Aerospace Forces: An Operational Architecture for Combat Support Execution Planning and Control*, James A. Leftwich, Robert S. Tripp, Amanda Geller, Patrick H. Mills, Tom LaTourrette, Charles Robert Roll, Jr., Cauley Von Hoffman, and David Johansen (MR-1536-AF). This report outlines the framework for evaluating options for combat support execution planning and control. The analysis describes the combat support C2 operational architecture as it is now, and as it should be in the future. It also describes the changes that must take place to achieve that future state.

- *Supporting Expeditionary Aerospace Forces: Lessons from Operation Enduring Freedom*, Robert S. Tripp, Kristin F. Lynch, John G. Drew, and Edward W. Chan (MR-1819-AF). This report describes the expeditionary ACS experiences during the war in Afghanistan and compares these experiences with those associated with JTF Noble Anvil, the air war over Serbia. This report analyzes how ACS concepts were implemented, compares current experiences to determine similarities and unique practices, and indicates how well the ACS framework performed during these contingency operations. From this analysis, the ACS framework may be updated to better support the AEF concept.

- *Supporting Expeditionary Aerospace Forces: Lessons from Operation Iraqi Freedom*, Kristin F. Lynch, John G. Drew, Robert S. Tripp, and Charles Robert Roll, Jr. (MG-193-AF). This monograph describes the expeditionary ACS experiences during the war in Iraq and compares these experiences with those associated with JTF Noble Anvil, in Serbia, and Operation Enduring Freedom, in Afghanistan. This report analyzes how combat support performed and how ACS concepts were implemented in Iraq, compares current experiences to determine similarities and unique practices, and indicates how well the ACS framework performed during these contingency operations.

RAND Project AIR FORCE

RAND Project AIR FORCE (PAF), a division of the RAND Corporation, is the U.S. Air Force's federally funded research and development center for studies and analyses. PAF provides the Air Force with independent analyses of policy alternatives affecting the development, employment, combat readiness, and support of current and future aerospace forces. Research is conducted in four programs: Force Modernization and Employment; Manpower, Personnel, and Training; Resource Management; and Strategy and Doctrine.

Additional information about PAF is available on our Web site:
http://www.rand.org/paf/

Contents

Preface iii

Figures ix

Tables xi

Summary xiii

Acknowledgments xix

Abbreviations xxi

CHAPTER ONE

Introduction, Motivation, and Approach 1

Study Motivation 1

Analytic Approach 2

CSC2 Case Studies 4

    Terminal Fury 2004 5

    Austere Challenge 2004 6

Organization of This Report 7

CHAPTER TWO

Combat Support Execution Planning Command and Control 9

CHAPTER THREE

Organizational Structure 13

Nodal Organization 14

    Case Study Findings 16

    Nodal Organization Implications 18

AOC Staffing and Organization 19

    Case Study Findings 19

    AOC Staffing Implications 20

CHAPTER FOUR

Command and Control Systems Integration and Decision-Support Tools 23

A Common Operating Picture 23

Case Study Findings...23
Common Operating Picture Implications...24
Exploiting Technology 25
Case Study Findings...25
Exploiting Technology Implications...26

CHAPTER FIVE
Training and Education...29
Implications...31

CHAPTER SIX
Summary Observations...33
Organizational Structure..34
C2 Systems Integration and Decision-Support Tools............................34
Training and Education..34

APPENDIXES
A. **Terminal Fury 2004 Case Study**...37
B. **Austere Challenge 2004 Case Study** 53
C. **Assessment Teams** 71

Bibliography...73

Figures

3.1.   TO-BE CSC2 Organizational Structure 14
3.2.   Terminal Fury 2004 Organizational Structure 17
3.3.   Austere Challenge 2004 Organizational Structure 17
3.4.   USAFE March 2004 Interim Organizational Construct 18
3.5.   Sample AOC Manning Levels, FY 2004 21
3.6.   Revised TO-BE CSC2 Operational Architecture 22
A.1.   TO-BE CSC2 Organizational Structure 39
A.2.   Terminal Fury 2004 Organizational Structure 40
A.3.   Terminal Fury 2004 AOC Organizational Structure 42
B.1.   TO-BE CSC2 Organizational Structure 55
B.2.   USAFE March 2004 Interim Organizational Construct 56
B.3.   Austere Challenge 2004 Organizational Structure 57

Tables

S.1. Areas of Assessment and Assessment Criteria xv
1.1. Areas of Assessment and Assessment Criteria 3
2.1. CSC2 Functionality Required to Meet AEF Operational Goals 9
2.2. TO-BE CSC2 Nodes and Responsibilities 11

Summary

In response to the CSC2 issues discovered during operations in Serbia in 1999, the Deputy Chief of Staff for Installations and Logistics (AF/IL) asked RAND PAF to study the current ("AS-IS") operational architecture and develop a future ("TO-BE") CSC2 operational architecture (Leftwich et al., 2002). PAF researchers documented current processes, identified areas in need of change, and developed processes for a well-defined, closed-loop TO-BE CSC2 operational architecture that incorporated the lessons learned during JTF Noble Anvil and Operation Enduring Freedom, which AF/IL directed for implementation.

The TO-BE operational architecture envisions enabling the ACS community to

- quickly estimate combat support requirements for force package options needed to achieve desired operational effects and assess the feasibility of operational and support plans
- quickly determine beddown capabilities, facilitate rapid time-phased force and deployment data (TPFDD) development, and configure a distribution network to meet employment time lines and resupply needs
- facilitate execution resupply planning and performance monitoring
- determine the effects of allocating scarce resources to various combatant commanders
- indicate when combat support performance deviates from the desired state and implement replanning and/or "get-well" planning analysis (Leftwich et al., 2002)
- provide decisionmakers with an Air Force–wide view of combat support resources available for joint employment operations.

The TO-BE architecture outlines changes in three key organizations: the Commander of Air Force forces' (COMAFFOR's) operations support center, commodity control points, and the Air Force Combat Support Center. It also affects operations occurring in the Falconer Air and Space Operations Center (AOC) weapon system and must work within the greater joint C2 environment.[1]

Two exercises provided opportunities to observe aspects of the TO-BE operational architecture currently in use in important CSC2 nodes in an operational environment: Terminal Fury 2004 (TF04) and Austere Challenge 2004 (AC04). A RAND team, aided by Air Force

---

[1] A Falconer AOC is one attached to a Combat Air Force warfighting headquarters and serves the COMAFFOR. The other type of AOC is a functional AOC, such as the Tanker Airlift Control Center, which is part of 18AF and collocated with the AMC staff. Generally, the term *AOC*, as used in this report, refers to the Falconer AOC weapon system.

personnel (see Appendix C for a list of the assessment team members), participated in TF04 and all three phases of AC04 to make these evaluations. The assessment teams used the operational environment created by TF04 and AC04 to observe CSC2 processes under stress.

The exercises offered opportunities to examine the extent to which an agile combat support–enabled (ACS-enabled) C2 structure can relate ACS actions to warfighter combat capability. Operational time lines have been collapsed to the point that the position and posture of combat support forces are key to delivery of desired combat power. As a consequence, combat support functional areas must work in an integrated fashion across C2 nodes, providing predictions of ACS needs and rapid ACS responses to dynamic operational needs.

In addition to the on-site assessment teams, PAF and Air Force participants gathered a group of strategic partners to review ACS activity daily, via teleconference. These partners represented the broader Air Force combat support community. They included personnel in theater and CONUS major commands, as well as personnel from Headquarters Air Force and support organizations. The group reviewed daily exercise activity and extrapolated off-site activity that would occur in the broader group of CSC2 nodes to support the warfighter combat force deployed within the context of the exercise. In this way, other Air Force nodes could participate in combat support activities that were not part of the overall exercise play. This capability complemented the aim of the research, which was to gain knowledge of the current ACS and operational-level C2 state-of-play and posture and to make observations regarding CSC2 resource and process strategy.

The aim of this research was to evaluate the progress the Air Force has made in implementing the TO-BE operational architecture and to identify areas that need additional improvements. Assessment team members were embedded during each exercise to observe CSC2 processes, such as the allocation of scarce resources, and to explore the integration of combat support systems and processes. Exercise limitations did not allow us to assess the closed-loop aspect of the CSC2 process, in which performance metrics and lessons learned lead to replanning of support.[2]

The exercises did point out areas where implementation of the TO-BE architecture is likely to produce major productivity gains and enhanced decisionmaking information as the Air Force continues to implement the architecture. Monitoring CSC2 processes, the assessment teams made observations in the following areas:

- implementation of proposed CSC2 organizations
  - organizational structure at various C2 nodes (between and within nodes)
  - AOC staffing and organization
- use of existing collaborative information systems and products
  - a common operating picture
  - exploiting technology
- efforts in training and education.

Table S.1 lists the assessment criteria used in each of the three areas.

---

[2] The exercise did not last long enough to require replanning of support.

Table S.1
Areas of Assessment and Assessment Criteria

Assessment Area	Criteria
Organizational structure	Who communicated with whom
	Method of communication
Systems and technology	Manual or electronic
	Common system or task-specific
Training and education	Method of training
	Amount of training

Agile CSC2 requires a support system that integrates combat support stovepipes and relates how options for providing support influence operational effects. ACS activity is an enabling function that shapes the combat power available to the joint force air component commander and the joint force commander at any given time. The ACS system postures forces for employment. Therefore, combat and supporting force commanders need an integrated C2 system to extend authority over forces used to achieve desired effects.

Exercise play was mined for situations in which the AS-IS operational architecture would be stressed. This provided the opportunity for the assessment team to look across nodes and within nodes (when assessment team members were available) to understand how ACS-engaged personnel processed exercise information to overcome problems and still achieve the desired combat effects. Particular attention was paid to how information was fed into operational-level CSC2 systems and shared across nodes. Discussions were initiated among the assessment team and with the strategic partners to improve understanding of how TO-BE processes, systems, and training would affect exercise play if fielded and in effect.

Terminal Fury 2004

In TF04, a PACOM-planned operational environment, force basing, logistics readiness, and force sustainment capabilities were critical factors of the joint force commander's ability to provide timely and sufficient force capability. To fulfill the TO-BE operational architecture, the ACS deliberate planning process should be fully integrated with the operational community's effort and harmonized with joint logistics planning processes. The operational architecture could facilitate the rapid creation of alternative courses of action that reflect needed capabilities and available forces for employment. Combat support planning tools, aimed at determining alternatives, could help make the support consequences of each course of action more visible to AOC planners, warfighting staff, and the joint force commanders they serve. An analytic CSC2 capability could help place these factors in an operational context. Identifying the potential constraints (such as host-nation infrastructure, alternative basing logistics time lines, force protection, and other joint force considerations) builds knowledge over the critical factors leading to building and fielding the desired capability. This could also shift the key information away from arrival of individual force components to the creation of actual combat capability and could help build command knowledge about what key factors are necessary to creating that capability. Enabled by the CSC2 TO-BE architecture, force arrival in theater would not be as important as when a specific capability becomes available for employment.

As a consequence of closer integration with operational planners in the A-3, A-5, and in the associated AOC, A-4, A-6, A-7, and other ACS functional elements may need to invest in the collaborative planning tools that are used in operational planning and execution.[3] Moving to a future force-planning environment means integrating ACS information systems and products. Once integrated, the information will help enable war-fighter decisions, gaining precision in force deployment and sustainment activity and helping shape the combat power available to the joint force commander.

During TF04, the limited first-generation collaborative planning tools (such as Information Workspace and Collaboration at Sea) that the operations cells forward (afloat) and in the rear used in the AOC may have helped reduce the time needed to work the problem. In moving from the AS-IS to the TO-BE CSC2 system, joint collaborative tools should be procured and widely distributed among all Air Force CSC2 nodes. CSC2 reporting systems should fully integrate with joint systems and incorporate inventory reporting systems with embedded machine-to-machine connections that will not only allow data owners to monitor and validate their data but, when tied to an information grid, will also allow increasingly accurate, commonly shared, and timely information flows to the force capability providers working directly with operational commanders. Personnel need to be trained in their use and educated about what the collaborative environment can provide. Collaborative tools and a shared data-entry system could have freed functional managers from compiling inventory reports on manual spreadsheets, improving their ability to monitor and direct the sustainment of forces flowing into the joint operating area. As base loading became critical during the second phase of operations, they would have a better knowledge base on which to project potential shortfalls and could have adjusted base force loads to sustain the needed warfighting capabilities better. The AS-IS system demands that these functional managers spend their time maintaining the data system. The TO-BE system will place a demand on their professional capabilities.

Austere Challenge 2004

In the AC04 operational environment, force basing, logistics readiness, and force sustainment capabilities were spread among AOC-like C2 and staff elements at several levels, including Combat Air Forces, Mobility Air Forces, and the deep strategic support capability vested in Air Force Materiel Command (AFMC), and among other organizations supporting the warfighting commands. However, most of this Air Force strategic support was outside the training audience. The exercise was aimed at testing the connection between the JTF air component in the forward area and the major command staff supporting and shaping the combat forces.

---

[3] For example, the necessary CSC2 systems and processes should be incorporated into the Falconer AOC and listed as appropriate in weapon system documentation, such as the Falconer AOC's *Flight Manual* (Falconer AOC, 2002).

The exercise was also being used by the USAFE Commander to validate a notional warfighting headquarters structure (the Air Force component for Europe [Air Forces Europe—AFEUR]) operating within a JTF.

The roles, missions, duties, and responsibilities of each of the C2 nodes were fairly well defined. Data collection and reporting and determining which information and which nodes were authoritative at both the tactical and theater levels caused some issues. Our observations found that physical location, on-site and face-to-face interaction are valued when the situation is less defined or when communications nodes are less robust.

Theater nodes that exercise control functions quickly adapted the structure for delivering their exercise products. The structure supported the operational context and the desire to share information files across nodes. The only cost was in the intellectual capital and keyboard man-hours used to create, structure, and maintain the workspace. This was an example of what can be accomplished given the current AS-IS architecture.

An investment should be made in CSC2 education to help define the desired work process, systems, and infrastructure requirements. Increased emphasis on obtaining and using collaborative tools would increase efficiencies and effectiveness until future network-centric solutions are developed.

Summary Observations

Monitoring CSC2 processes, such as how combat support requirements for force package options needed to achieve desired operational effects were developed, the assessment teams made observations in three areas: organizational structure, systems and tools, and training and education. While the research presented here took place in 2004, a number of our findings are still relevant today. The following is a summary of the observations the assessment teams made during their 2004 exercise experiences.

Organizational Structure

Differing organizational constructs exist today. Some of these may be fine-tuned for different operational environments. As long as the roles and responsibilities are well defined, the organizational structure should not have a large effect:

- Air Force CSC2 nodes should fully understand their roles and authority when working with warfighting headquarters.
- Warfighting headquarters should learn—through common practice—the value of Air Force service-led support.
- All organizations should share information with appropriate CSC2 nodes.
- Within the theater, each organizational node should understand and execute its responsibilities within the tasked operational authority. (Theaterwide capability must work to enable CSC2 capabilities assigned to a JTC with specific joint tasks to perform.)

- We suggest that a logistics component be matrixed across AOC divisions to provide combat support expertise and eliminate a parallel C2 structure in the warfighting headquarters staff.

C2 Systems Integration and Decision-Support Tools

A common information management architecture could be defined so that each node is working from common information:

- An information management plan could be developed for managing the common system architecture so that a common operating picture can be developed.
- ACS systems and processes should be integrated to operational systems at the data level.

Technology should be exploited to allow sharing of information through Web-based tools, Really Simple Syndication (RSS)–enabled data and text streams, and automatic data builds for decisionmaker viewing (instead of building slides). Using technology to share common data should allow more time for "what if" analysis and resource allocation, and less time will be spent generating Microsoft PowerPoint slides.

Training and Education

Exercises should be designed to engage all nodes in the ACS arena:

- Provide an opportunity to work across nodes in a collaborative environment.
- Construct Blue Flag exercises to engage ACS personnel.
- Develop a strategy to involve key CONUS CSC2 nodes in theater C2 exercises.
- Continue to manage functional career areas to acquire the deep knowledge necessary to perform with the precision needed in fielding and sustaining combat forces.
  - Develop an appreciation for operational risk as it applies to providing forces.
  - Develop fluency with modeling and simulation of ACS activity to better influence operational outcomes to meet desired effects during force structure beddown and planning.
- Build the means for building knowledge of best practices across ACS for the entire Air Force.
- Teach ACS critical thinking and problem-solving in an operational environment.

Invest in the education of personnel who understand ACS functional areas, but learn how to best leverage technology and TO-BE information management processes.

Acknowledgments

Many individuals in the Air Force provided valuable assistance and support to our work. We thank Maj Gen Craig Rasmussen, Director of Logistics Readiness (AF/ILG), for sponsoring this analysis and Brig Gen Ronald Ladnier for continuing it. We thank Lt Gen Donald Wetekam for helping focus the project and providing support within AF/IL. We also thank Gen William Begert, Commander, Pacific Air Forces, and Gen Robert Foglesong, Commander, U.S. Air Forces in Europe, for allowing us to conduct assessments in their theaters.

We are especially grateful for the support we received from Headquarters, Air Force, specifically Col Connie Morrow, AF/ILGX, and her staff. On our assessment teams, we thank Lt Col Kimberlee Zorich, Jaime Santana, and Freddie McSears, Sr., from AF/ILGX; Lt Col Bruce Springs from the Combat Support Center; and Lt Col Carl Zimmerman from the Air Force Command and Control, Intelligence, Surveillance, and Reconnaissance Center (AFC2ISRC).

We also thank our strategic partners for participating in these assessments. Specifically, we thank Capt Sheldon Werner, USAFE LG/LGXE; Maj Tracey Birri, AFMC/LSO LOR; SMSgt Lawrence January, AMC; and Lt Col David Terry and James Denkert from AFC2ISRC. We also thank Margaret Timmons and James Welshans, 505 OS/OCTP, for providing insight on training and education.

Acknowledgments from PACAF

We are grateful to Brig Gen Polly Peyer, PACAF/LG; Col Kurt Grabey, Commander, 502 Air and Space Operations Squadron; and Col Russell Grunch, PACAF/LGX-ALOC. General Peyer, Colonel Grabey, and Colonel Grunch all provided the assessment team free and open access to everyone under their commands.

This assessment would not have been possible without the help and support of the staffs of the Thirteenth Air Force (13AF), the PACAF Operations Support Center (POSC), the AOC, and the PACAF/LG-ALOC. In particular, from 13AF, we would like to thank Col Gregg Sanders, 13AF Vice Commander; Lt Col Richard Baldwin and Maj James Wingo, Jr., 13AF CAT Directors; Maj Brian Rusler, A-4; Maj Robert Harrington, A-6; and CMSgt (Select) Brian Nornback, A-4.3.

At Hickam AFB, Hawaii, we would like to thank Capt Myron Shirley and TSgt Maryrose McGhee in the POSC; Lt Col Mark Jones and MSgt Brad Harris in the AOC; and especially Lt Col Ted Pierson, CMSgt Davis DuFour, Capt Christopher Afful, and Capt Adrian Crowley in the PACAF-LG/ALOC. Captain Afful and Colonel Gabey helped during the early days of the research process in working with AF/IL in crafting the study and making suggestions on how best to position the assessment team during TF04. The early and continued support from PACAF/DO (Air Operations Group) and LG senior leaders was much appreciated.

Acknowledgments from USAFE

We are grateful to Brig Gen (Select) Jay Lindell, USAFE/A-4; Col Michael Isherwood, AFEUR Vice Commander; and Col Steven J. Depalmer, Commander, 32 Air Operations Group. Their units provided the core personnel in the exercise training audience for AC04. General Lindell, Colonel Isherwood, and Colonel Depalmer all provided the assessment team free and open access to everyone under their commands.

This assessment would not have been possible without the help and support of the Sixteenth Air Force (16AF) staff, the AFEUR, the AOC, and the USAFE Headquarters staff. In particular, we would like to thank Lt Gen Glen Moorhead III, 16AF Commander, Col John E. Julsonnet, Capt Peter Abercrombie, Capt Joyce Storm, and Maj Douglas Meikle, all of 16AF/A-4.

There are a number of people we would like to thank at Ramstein Air Base, Germany. We would like to thank Col John McKoy, Lt Col Bryan Glynn, Maj Michael Araujo, Maj Curtis Iszard, and Kent Reedy in the AFEUR and Lt Col Bryan Edmonds, Lt Col Kevin Walsh (152 AOG), Lt Col Ronald Yakkel, and Maj Marc Jamison for help in the AOC. We also thank TSgt Lynn deHaan, 32 AOG; TSgt David Paddock, 152 AOG; Lt Col Craig Donnely, Deputy Chief of Combat Plans; and Maj Michael Comella, 152 AOG, for sharing their knowledge and Col John Snider, Col Harry Teti, Col Charlie Weiss, Lt Col Jack Patterson, Capt Scott Burroughs, and Capt U. Ita Udoaka for their assistance.

And we especially thank Lt Col Eric Jacobson, Capt Shelton Werner, CMSgt Daniel Owens, SMSgt Samuel Graves, and Ed Santos for all their help during our visits. Captain Shelton and Colonel Jacobson also contributed during the initial period of the research, making key suggestions about structuring observations and projecting where TO-BE activity would have the greatest influence on ACS activity. Their contact, intellectual energy, and optimism during the research greatly aided the CSC2 effort.

Finally, at RAND, we enhanced our analysis through the knowledge and support of many of our colleagues, especially John Drew, Robert Tripp, Patrick Mills, and Charles Robert Roll, Jr. We would also like to thank John Bondanella and David Shlapak for their thorough review of this report. Their reviews helped shape this document into its final, improved form. Special thanks to Darlette Gayle, Angela Holmes, and Dahlia Lichter for their tireless support of this project.

Abbreviations

11AF	Eleventh Air Force
13AF	Thirteenth Air Force
16AF	Sixteenth Air Force
A-1	Manpower and Personnel
A-2	Intelligence
A-3	Operations
A-4	Logistics
A-5	Plans
A-6	Communications and Information
A-7	Installations and Mission Support
A-8	Programs and Financial Management
A-9	Analyses, Assessments and Lessons Learned
AB	air base
AC04	Austere Challenge 2004
ACS	agile combat support
AEF	air and space expeditionary force
AF/IL	Deputy Chief of Staff for Installations and Logistics
AF/ILG	Directorate of Logistics Readiness
AF/ILGX	Directorate of Logistics Readiness, ACS Doctrine and Wargames Division
AFB	Air Force base

AFC2ISRC	Air Force Command and Control, Intelligence, Surveillance, and Reconnaissance Center
AFEUR	Air Forces Europe
AFFOR	Air Force forces
AFMC	Air Force Materiel Command
AIG	Air Intelligence Group
AMC	Air Mobility Command
AMOCC	Air Mobility Operations Control Center
AOC	Air and Space Operations Center
AOG	Air and Space Operations Group
AOR	area of responsibility
APOSC	Asia Pacific Operations Support Center
ASETF	air and space expeditionary task force
A-staff	AFFOR staff
ATO	air tasking order
C2	command and control
CAF	Combat Air Forces
CAMS	Core Automated Maintenance System
CAS	Collaboration at Sea
CAT	crisis action team
CC	commander
CCP	commodity control point
COA	course of action
COMAFFOR	Commander of Air Force forces
COMPACAF	Commander, Pacific Air forces
CONOPS	concept of operations
CONUS	continental United States
CPT	contingency planning team
CSAF	Chief of Staff, U.S. Air Force

CSC	combat support center
CSC2	combat support execution planning and control
D/COMAFFOR	Deputy Commander of Air Force forces
DCAPES	Deliberate and Crisis Planning and Execution Segments
ECS	expeditionary combat support
EOC	expeditionary operations center
ESP2	Expeditionary Site Planning Portal
EUCOM	U.S. European Command
FY	fiscal year
HQ	headquarters
IG	inspector general
IM	information management
IRC	Installation Readiness Cell
ISR	intelligence, surveillance, and reconnaissance
IWS	Information Workspace
JAOC	Joint Air and Space Operations Center
JFACC	joint force air component commander
JFC	joint forces commander
JOA	joint operating area
JOAP	joint air operations planning
JOPES	Joint Operations Planning and Execution System
J-staff	Joint Staff
JTF	joint task force
LNO	liaison officer
LOGCROP	Logistics Common Relevant Operational Picture
LPT	logistics planning team
LRC	Logistics Readiness Center
MAAP	master air attack plan

MAF	Mobility Air Forces
MAJCOM	major command
NAF	numbered air force
NATO	North Atlantic Treaty Organization
NCO	noncommissioned officer
NIPRNET	Nonsecure Internet Protocol Router Network
OSC	operations support center
PACAF	U.S. Pacific Air Forces
PACOM	U.S. Pacific Command
PED	processing, exploitation, and dissemination
POSC	PACAF Operations Support Center
RSS	Really Simple Syndication
SIPRNET	Secure Internet Protocol Router Network
SITREP	situation report
SMS	single mobility system
STE	secure telephone equipment
STU III	secure telephone unit
TBMCS	Theater Battle Management Core System
TDS	theater distribution system
TF04	Terminal Fury 2004
TPFDD	time-phased force and deployment data
USAFE	U.S. Air Forces in Europe
UTASC	USAFE Theater Aerospace Support Center
UTC	unit type code
WPC	Warfighter Preparation Center
XML	Extensible Markup Language

CHAPTER ONE

Introduction, Motivation, and Approach

A rapidly changing security environment and increasing demands for Air Force support have led the Air Force to transition into an air and space expeditionary force (AEF). AEF goals emphasize agility, precision, and speed—the ability to immediately deploy, employ, and sustain fighting forces anywhere in the world. A combatant commander may employ forces from major commands (MAJCOMs), numbered air forces (NAFs), and many different wings and units. That combatant commander needs strong control over these assigned and supporting forces. Agile combat support (ACS) concepts (such as just-in-time delivery, force beddown planning, and theater distribution system [TDS] network analysis) shape combat power within a given set of available resources. An ACS system postures forces for combat employment. With more-precise and timely information about forces, supporting infrastructure, materiel inventories, movement capabilities, and the warfighters' desired effects, personnel working combat support tasks may be able to provide and sustain forces more effectively and efficiently. Combat and supporting force commanders need an integrated command and control (C2) system to extend authority over all forces building for any desired effect.

Study Motivation

During operations in Serbia and Afghanistan, combat support execution planning and control (CSC2) was developed on an ad hoc basis and did not always follow doctrine (Tripp et al., 2004). Processes were essentially manual and generally involved person-to-person exchanges of information, such as email messages or telephone calls. In response to the CSC2 issues discovered during the air war over Serbia, the Deputy Chief of Staff for Installations and Logistics (AF/IL) chartered a RAND Corporation analysis of the current ("AS-IS") CSC2 operational architecture and the development of a future ("TO-BE") CSC2 operational architecture.

Over the course of two years, the RAND CSC2 analysis documented the current processes, identified areas in need of change, and developed processes for a well-defined, closed-loop TO-BE CSC2 operational architecture incorporating the lessons learned during recent operations.[1] The TO-BE architecture defines CSC2 processes and the associated roles and

---

[1] A *closed-loop* process takes the output and uses it as an input for the next iteration of the process.

responsibilities. More detail on CSC2 and the TO-BE operational architecture is provided in Chapter Two of this report.[2]

C2 systems that expand the commander's view are not just created to perform set tasks but are expected to respond and adapt to a changing operational environment. The CSC2 capability must not only serve the commander but must also interact across nodes. It is not about technology but about determining what each node needs, assessing work processes, and then providing the technology and human interaction that will add value either to the substance or by easing the ability of people to maintain their situational awareness and make informed decisions. Observation and feedback are integral to fielding a TO-BE operational architecture that makes sense to future users.

AF/IL directed the ACS community to begin implementing the designs from the TO-BE CSC2 operational architecture. Roles and responsibilities are being tied to specific organizations. Air Force Doctrine Document 2-4, Combat Support, is in review and ACS changes are currently being incorporated as of this writing. Likewise, more attention is being paid to the ACS component within C2 systems, such as the Falconer Air and Space Operations Center (AOC).[3]

While the research presented in this report was conducted in 2004 and the Air Force CSC2 system continues to evolve, a number of the findings from participation in these exercises are still applicable today.

Analytic Approach

As the Air Force began to transition to the TO-BE CSC2 operational architecture, the Directorate of Logistics Readiness (AF/ILG) was tasked to assess the implementation. AF/ILG asked RAND Project AIR FORCE to help in this evaluation. Two annual command post exercises provided opportunities to observe aspects of the TO-BE operational architecture currently in use in important CSC2 nodes in an operational environment: Terminal Fury 2004 (TF04), a Pacific Command (PACOM) exercise held in December 2003, and Austere Challenge 2004 (AC04), a U.S. Air Forces, Europe (USAFE) exercise held January through March 2004. A RAND team, aided by Air Force personnel, participated in TF04 and all three phases of AC04. (See Appendix C for a list of assessment team members for each exercise.) The exercises themselves were not the focus of the assessment. The assessment teams used the operational environments created by TF04 and AC04 to observe CSC2 processes under stress.

The primary objective of the assessment was to evaluate the extent to which the Air Force was transitioning to the TO-BE CSC2 architecture and to identify areas of the TO-BE operational architecture that needed additional improvements. Members of the assessment team

---

[2] For an in-depth review of the initial study, see Leftwich et al. (2002).

[3] A Falconer AOC is attached to a Combat Air Forces (CAF) warfighting headquarters and serves the Commander of Air Force forces (COMAFFOR). The other type of AOC is a functional AOC, such as the Tanker Airlift Control Center, which is part of 18th Air Force and collocated with the Air Mobility Command (AMC) staff. Generally, the term *AOC*, as used in this report, refers to the Falconer AOC weapon system.

were embedded in participating theater units during each exercise to observe CSC2 processes, such as the allocation of scarce resources, and to explore the integration of combat support systems and processes with operational systems and processes. The assessment team reviewed what would be necessary to take the observed processes between combat support nodes, such as the HQ USAF Combat Support Center (AF CSC), an operations support center (OSC), the AOC, and the joint task force (JTF), and move them toward the TO-BE operational architecture. Exercise limitations did not allow the assessment team to evaluate the closed loop aspect of the CSC2 process, in which performance metrics and lessons learned lead to replanning of support.[4] Monitoring CSC2 processes, the assessment team made observations in the following areas:

- organizational structure
- use of collaborative information systems and products
- efforts in training and education.

Table 1.1 lists the assessment criteria used in each of the three areas.

Using CSC2 processes, such as how combat support requirements for force package options needed to achieve desired operational effects were developed, as a guide, the assessment team evaluated nodal processes (who communicated with whom and how), both across and within nodes; how information flowed (manually or electronically); what systems were used (common or task-specific systems); and how personnel were prepared for their positions (training and education).

The assessment was conducted on a noninterference basis; the assessment team observed but did not change the exercise activity in any way. RAND personnel were allowed access to exercise scenarios in advance to help the assessment team plan the placement of its members and to schedule participation. These observations were not limited to systems but attempted

Table 1.1
Areas of Assessment and Assessment Criteria

Assessment Area	Criteria
Organizational structure	Who communicated with whom
	Method of communication
Systems and technology	Manual or electronic
	Common system or task-specific
Training and education	Method of training
	Amount of training

---

[4] The closed-loop methodology of planning, measuring, executing, assessing, and adjusting is central to the TO-BE operational architecture. However, the exercise did not last long enough to require replanning of support.

to encompass doctrine; operational interfaces; and effects on desired capabilities, training and education, materiel, equipment, process organization, and leadership.[5]

The research process was structured to include many of the Air Force organizations responsible for CSC2 nodes to help build, if not an institutional consensus, at least greater understanding and a common vocabulary for these personnel. In addition to the on-site assessment team, RAND Project AIR FORCE and Air Force participants gathered a group of strategic partners daily, via teleconference, to review ACS activity during both exercises. Personnel at the AF CSC, the Air Force Materiel Command (AFMC), AMC, and the Air Force Command and Control Intelligence, Surveillance, and Reconnaissance Center (AFC2ISRC) were contacted about exercise-generated activity to investigate potential effects on these Air Force nodes, thus serving as strategic partners in the analysis. During the daily teleconferences, issues the exercise scenario did not cover could be discussed and, in some cases, worked independently as homework for the strategic partners. This allowed a much wider group to observe, and in some cases participate, in a way that did not interfere with theater exercise goals and objectives. It also brought Air Force functional leadership into the exercise environment, albeit in a limited way.

CSC2 Case Studies

This report is not an assessment of the exercises but rather a review of the CSC2 architecture in use today and an evaluation of the progress toward the future, TO-BE, operational architecture. The exercises offered opportunities to observe ACS tasks within the operational context of a major C2 theater exercise. Each exercise provided a unique opportunity to observe a range of CSC2 nodes involved in executing the scenario, such as a COMAFFOR/Joint Force Air Component Commander (JFACC), a notional Air Force forces (AFFOR) staff (the engaged NAF), the AOC, and MAJCOM theaterwide organizations. The exercise scenario involved forces from both CAF and mobility air forces (MAF) providers with MAF and sustainment elements embedded in the AOC and AFFOR staff organizations.

Both exercises were limited to the scenario as scripted. The exercise goals and theater objectives were outside the scope of this study, but they did provide a robust joint operational environment that generated a wealth of ACS inputs and outcomes. Organizational challenges for personnel employed in ACS activities were created in each scenario that may be unique to that theater and may therefore not apply to other theaters. When appropriate, the assessment teams identified such unique issues. Regionally specific exercises traditionally do not include all the participants required to assess the total ACS design. However, as noted above, the research design did include a role for CSC2 strategic partners in which issues the exercise scenario did not cover could be discussed and, in some cases, worked independently. The goal was to be in

---

[5]   Department of Defense organizations refer to these contributing elements—doctrine, organization, training, materiel, leadership, and personnel—as "DOTMLP." The assessment team found the contributing elements in AC04 for CSC2 broader than this list of factors and, where appropriate, related comments to the affected elements specifically rather than generally to DOTMLP.

a position to make informed assessments about the exercise activity—how information moved through CSC2 nodes and what could be done to gain knowledge about and insights into improving the Air Force ACS community's movement to the TO-BE CSC2 architecture.

The static assessment of movement toward the TO-BE CSC2 operational architecture during TF04 and AC04 was successful. The assessment teams learned how operational commands were organized and how they were performing ACS activities, documenting what exists today. The assessors attempted to capture and document this tacit knowledge when possible.[6]

Terminal Fury 2004

Sponsored by PACOM, Terminal Fury is an annual C2 exercise designed to rehearse a PACOM operational plan or potential course of action (COA). Terminal Fury 2004 (TF04) took place in December 2003. The CSC2 assessment team did not change the exercise scenario or alter PACOM and Pacific Air Forces (PACAF) exercise goals. This exercise included CSC2 nodes, such as a JTF headquarters staff, a COMAFFOR/JFACC, an AFFOR staff (the engaged NAF, Thirteenth Air Force [13AF], with elements afloat and in garrison), the AOC (including afloat and rear elements tasked to support the JFACC[7]), and MAJCOM theater reachback (the PACAF OSC [POSC]) within the exercise training audience.

TF04 was a PACOM command post exercise, not a field exercise. Organizations above or outside PACOM's area of responsibility (AOR) and forces below the operational level did not participate.[8] Specifically, the training audience consisted of the exercise PACOM commander and staff; the standing JTF 519 commander and staff (which served as the tasked JTF); service components (such as PACAF); their operational-level C2 nodes; and the JTF land, sea, and air component staffs that were created for the exercise around the standing JTF 519. Because of this level of participation, inputs above and below the theater and force levels were simulated; certain functions were not performed; and/or scripted responses were given to queries.

Generally, issues and problems were worked within specific functional areas at each location. Effort and task integration was coordinated at a higher level. Sometimes this resulted in parallel taskings. Coordination between nodes occurred primarily between like functional specialties (for example, fuels, munitions). Sometimes the issue or problem was reported during a node's daily or situation briefing, during which other functional areas could become aware of the tasking.

Given the specific TF04 scenario, exercise objectives, and timing for observations, the assessment team anticipated a focus on force beddown planning and execution and on force sustainment (for example, such commodities as fuel and munitions). Using these topics as a focus, the assessment team reviewed how information flowed between nodes, as well as within nodes; what systems were used; and how training was provided for personnel involved in the topic of focus. However, because of limitations in the TF04 exercise design, the assessment

---

[6] The tacit information is internal to the group of personnel performing the manual processes.

[7] During TF04, the AOC was not physically collocated with the JFACC.

[8] There were a few exceptions to this, but they did not significantly affect the CSC2 observations. CSC2 observers did engage other Air Force nodes, but these were not part of the PACOM exercise.

team was not able to assess all CSC2 nodes.[9] The primary focus became the COMAFFOR OSC's interaction with the AOC and reachback theater capabilities (13AF-to-PACAF POSC and AOC). More information about the TF04 case study can be found in Appendix B.

Austere Challenge 2004

The Chairman of the Joint Chiefs of Staff sponsored AC04. The exercise was directed and scheduled by the U.S. European Command (EUCOM) and conducted by USAFE as a warfighting exercise. Austere Challenge 2004 (AC04) took place January through March 2004. The exercise scenario and supporting simulated environment were developed and run by the Warfighter Preparation Center (WPC) facility at Einsedlerhof Air Station near Ramstein Air Base (AB), Germany, which is jointly maintained by USAFE and the U.S. Army Europe Command.[10] A C2 exercise, Austere Challenge was designed to exercise a USAFE operational plan or potential COA. A range of CSC2 nodes was involved in executing the scenario, including a COMAFFOR/JFACC, an AFFOR staff (the engaged NAF, Sixteenth Air Force [16AF]), the AOC, and the MAJCOM theaterwide organization (Air Forces Europe [AFEUR]). In addition to the exercise goals, the USAFE Commander asked the USAFE Inspector General (IG) to help validate the AFEUR organization and tasks, a notional warfighting headquarters structure operating within a JTF. The JTF air component structure was supported by a theaterwide COMAFFOR staff.

AC04 was a USAFE command post exercise, not a field exercise. Organizations above or outside the USAFE MAJCOM and 16AF (the forward AFFOR) did not participate.[11] Forces below the operational level were simulated by the WPC. The training audience consisted of the JFACC and staff, AFFOR staff, AOC, and the AFEUR.[12] Because of this level of participation, force-level inputs were simulated, certain functions were not performed, and/or scripted responses were given to queries.

The AC04 exercise schedule was accelerated by a month and divided into three phases. In addition, some of the training audience's organizational structure (AFEUR) did not exist prior

---

[9] The JTF commander and staff and the component commanders and key staff were deployed on a naval vessel. CSC2 observation relied on daily commander teleconferences and on PACAF personnel deployed on board the vessel as JTF/J-4 or component staff. Bandwidth limitations made it very difficult to stay in regular contact with these personnel.

[10] The exercise was split into three phases, and the later phases were gradually shifted to a more air-centric scenario.

[11] There were representatives of the other EUCOM service commands and the North Atlantic Treaty Organization (NATO). Their participation was limited to the context of the training audience. WPC- or Air Force–provided role players simulated the participation of JTFs, EUCOM, national leadership, and other JTF components.

[12] The AFEUR is a new organizational construct tied to the future warfighting headquarters initiative. The core of the AFEUR originated in the former USAFE Theater Aerospace Support Center (UTASC) augmented by functional areas from the USAFE staff. The AFEUR was designed to be the theaterwide provider of forces for this exercise commanded by a general officer reporting to the USAFE Commander.

to the exercise. Personnel had to be identified, trained, and quickly inserted into the exercise warfighting structure.[13]

Because the exercise schedule was accelerated, assessment team members did not have a separate orientation session with USAFE. However, during the first two exercise phases, assessment team members did meet with functional area supervisors, commanders, and special agencies (for example, USAFE/IG and the AFEUR vice commander) with a role in ACS or exercise analysis activity. Like PACAF, USAFE is functionally organized with the AFEUR, serving as an OSC. Unlike PACAF, USAFE was supporting Operation Iraqi Freedom during this period, and some functional managers were deployed. As a consequence of this and the accelerated schedule, there were fewer opportunities to meet and discuss the AS-IS with USAFE functional managers.

Given the specific AC04 scenario, exercise objectives, and timing for observations, the anticipated focus of the assessment team was on force beddown planning and deployment during Phase II of the exercise (February 2004) and on force execution and sustainment during Phase III of the exercise (March 2004). As during TF04, the assessment team used these targeted areas of interest to review organizational structure, systems and technology, and training. However, because of limitations in the AC04 exercise design, the primary focus became the AFFOR's interaction with the AOC and reachback to the headquarters theater capability to support or shape the combat force assigned to the joint forces commander (JFC). More information about the AC04 case study can be found in Appendix C.

Organization of This Report

This report begins by providing some CSC2 background in Chapter Two. In Chapter Three, we look at organizational structure. In Chapter Four, we look at information systems and support tools. Chapter Five focuses on training and education. The final chapter, Chapter Six, summarizes our conclusions and recommendations. Appendix A presents in-depth information about TF04, as does Appendix B about AC04. Appendix C lists the assessment team members for both exercises.

---

[13] This was one reason the USAFE commander split the exercise into three phases, in the hope that personnel tasked for Phase I would return for following phases. This did not always happen, creating a train-as-you-go environment that allowed some personnel working ACS tasks to establish their own, sometimes unique, work processes—especially in the new organizations.

CHAPTER TWO

Combat Support Execution Planning Command and Control

Since 1997, RAND has studied AEF operational goals and options for an ACS system needed to support them. A vital part of any ACS system is CSC2. Table 2.1 lists several AEF operational needs and the CSC2 requirements for supporting them.

In 2002, concentrating on CSC2 and combat support warfighting tasks, RAND evaluated the existing (AS-IS) CSC2 operational architecture. Evaluating CSC2 processes revealed shortfalls in organizational structure, information systems and tools, and training and education (Leftwich, et al., 2002). By comparing lessons learned from operations in Serbia (and, more recently, in Afghanistan and Iraq) with expected functionality, a future (TO-BE) CSC2 operational architecture was defined.

Table 2.1
CSC2 Functionality Required to Meet AEF Operational Goals

AEF Operational Need	CSC2 Requirement
Rapidly tailor force packages to achieve desired operational effects	Estimate combat support requirements for suitable force package options
	Assess feasibility of alternative operational and support plans
	Identify and preplan potential operating locations
Deploy rapidly	Determine forward operating location beddown capabilities and capacities for force packages
	Facilitate rapid time-phased force and deployment data (TPFDD) development
Employ quickly	Configure distribution network rapidly to meet employment tasking and resupply needs
Shift to sustainment smoothly	Execute resupply plans
	Monitor performance
Allocate scarce resources where they are needed most	Determine effects of allocating scarce resources to various combatant commanders
	Prioritize allocations to users
Adapt to changes quickly	Indicate when combat support performance deviates from desired state
	Facilitate development and implementation of "get-well" plans

SOURCE: Leftwich et al. (2002).

As part of the Air Force CSC2 TO-BE operational architecture, nodal responsibilities were refined and assigned to existing organizations.[1] Table 2.2 presents the CSC2 nodal responsibilities and processes outlined in the TO-BE operational architecture. By assigning roles and responsibilities to existing organizations, CSC2 should be better able to support AEF operational objectives: rapidly deploying, employing, and sustaining aerospace power globally.

The purpose of this study was to evaluate Air Force movement toward the CSC2 TO-BE operational architecture. By looking at CSC2 processes, we evaluate the previously identified shortfalls in organizational structure, information systems and tools, and training and education.

---

[1] A node is a point of intersection, within a larger infrastructure, at which the integration of processes and information occurs.

Table 2.2
TO-BE CSC2 Nodes and Responsibilities

CSC2 Nodes	Roles and Responsibilities
Joint staff	
Logistics Readiness Center (LRC)	Arbitrates supply and demand across combatant commands
Combatant command	
LRC	Provides combatant command logistics guidance and COA analysis
Joint Movement Center	Arbitrates supply of and demand for transportation
Joint Petroleum Office	Arbitrates supply of and demand for petroleum, oil, and lubricants
Joint Facilities Utilization Board	Arbitrates supply of and demand for facilities and real estate
Joint Materiel Priorities and Allocation Board	Arbitrates supply of and demand for materiel
JTF	
JTF J-4 and LRC	Provide JTF logistics guidance
	Arbitrate supply and demand among service components within the JTF
JFACC	
Joint air and space operations center combat support representatives	Support joint air operations planning and master air attack plan (MAAP) and air tasking order (ATO) production
JFACC staff logisticians	Provide JFACC logistics guidance
Air Force	
AF CSC	Monitors operations
	Represents Air Force combat support interests to the Joint Staff
	Conducts and reviews assessments of integrated weapon systems and base operating support
	Arbitrates supply of and demand for critical resources in short supply across AFFORs
AFFOR	
AOC combat support element	Supports joint air operations planning and MAAP and ATO production
AFFOR A-4 staff (forward)	Conducts site surveys and plans beddowns
	Provides liaison with AOC combat support element
AFFOR A-4 staff (rear)[a]	Assesses mission and sortie capabilities
	Assesses beddown and infrastructure requirements
	Assesses air and space expeditionary task force (ASETF) force structure support requirements
	Arbitrates supply and demand within ASETF among AEFs and bases
	Plans theater distribution system requirements
	Provides force closure analysis
	Provides liaison with Air Mobility Division in AOC
	Provides liaison with theater U.S. Transportation Command node

Table 2.2—Continued

CSC2 Nodes	Roles and Responsibilities
Deployed units	
Wing Operations Center	Disseminates unit tasking
	Reports unit status
CSC	Monitors and reports performance and inventory status
Supporting commands[b]	
LRC/CSC	Monitors unit deployments
	Allocates resources to resolve deploying unit shortfalls
Deploying units	
Wing Operations Center	Reports unit status
	Disseminates unit tasking
Deployment Control Center	Plans and executes wing deployment
	Reports status of deployment
Commodity control points (CCPs)	
Munitions; spares; petroleum, oil, and lubricants; bare base equipment; rations; medical materiel; etc.	Monitor resource levels
	Assess depot and/or contractor capabilities
	Work with the AF CSC to allocate resources according to theater and global priorities
Sources of supply[c]	
Command centers	Monitor production performance and report capacity

[a] The personnel at an OSC that supports forward AFFOR A-4 staff.
[b] The force and sustainment providers.
[c] The depots, commercial suppliers, etc.

Organizational Structure

In observing the two exercises, TF04 and AC04, the objective was to assess Air Force ACS use of the TO-BE nodes of the CSC2 operational architecture and its current effectiveness.[1] This TO-BE operational architecture refers to key communications and ACS work centers as *nodes*. Also, the Air Force component-level or operational-level C2 has produced a C2 weapon system, the AOC. The AOC is primarily the responsibility of the COMAFFOR that it serves; however, it can also be referred to as a "J," for *joint*, AOC if it supports a COMAFFOR who is also a JFACC. Likewise, if the operational-level commander is commanding a coalition force with air forces from more than one country, it can be designated as a "C," for *coalition*, AOC. At the foundation of all these is the COMAFFOR's AOC.

The AOC is process-organized, focused on producing formal war plans, such as an ATO, then using them to employ forces to achieve the JFC's desired strategic and tactical objectives.[2] The COMAFFOR/JFACC relies on his assigned combat force CSC2 personnel, working with his headquarters staff and with theater and service support forces and organizations, to shape and posture the combat power available for employment.

The TO-BE operational architecture also refers to intersections between ACS-engaged organizations as nodes. This allowed the assessment team to look at ACS as an information-sharing network. The assessment structure we put into place included a forward assessment team observing the AOC and other theater exercise CSC2 nodes and others (called strategic partners) monitoring CONUS-based support organizations. Each node generally had a formal name (for example, POSC), but most are ad hoc, formed with very specific local tasks and performance expectations. As the Air Force moves toward the TO-BE, these nodes, with clearly defined roles and responsibilities, should be further developed. During the two exercises, we observed nodes within AOCs and within staff organizations and support organizations.

Chapter Three discusses the following areas:

- nodal organization
- AOC staffing and organization.

---

[1] This notional architecture was accepted by the Air Force and provides the basis for the TO-BE architecture the AF/IL directed to be implemented. See *Air Force Journal of Logistics* (2003), for more implementation information.

[2] The JFACC works directly for the JFC and employs assigned forces. The COMAFFOR advises the JFC on the use of Air Force forces and may be designated as the JFFAC.

Nodal Organization

The AF/IL CSC2 TO-BE architecture provides an organizational construct to ensure C2 that functions are performed through a standard or uniform arrangement of personnel, equipment, communications, facilities, and procedures throughout the Air Force. We need to point out that this research was conducted during a period of transition for the Air Force—a transition to a new warfighting headquarters structure. This transition affected CSC2 organizational nodes. Likewise, the lessons from Operations Enduring Freedom and Iraqi Freedom emphasized the importance of the role of the COMAFFOR and showed that its role was not fully understood across the Air Force (Tripp et al., 2004; Lynch et al., 2005). Figure 3.1 illustrates the suggested nodes in the TO-BE CSC2 operational architecture when the assessment began. As a notional construct, it illustrates the various community players and the context of their organizational placement.

The CSC2 construct, if the COMAFFOR employs it, enables planning, directing, coordinating, and controlling forces and combat support operations, taking the role of a service component to the JFC. The primary focus of the assessment was the COMAFFOR/JFACC and the nodes he or she employed.

The first node considered consisted of the COMAFFOR, the JFACC, and their staffs (labeled 1 in Figure 3.1). The COMAFFOR is responsible for all Air Force forces, including assets and personnel. The JFACC is responsible for employing all air assets, including Navy air assets. In most cases, the COMAFFOR is dual-hatted as the JFACC, but that might not

Figure 3.1
TO-BE CSC2 Organizational Structure

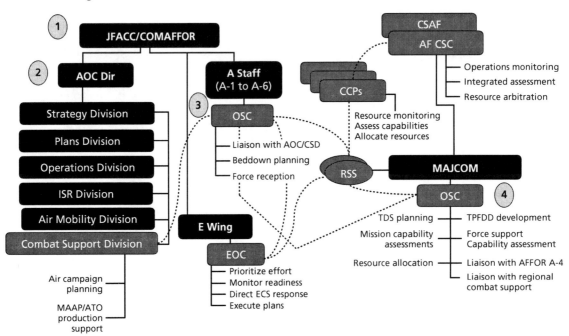

RAND TR356-3.1

always be the case. The JFACC could be a naval officer aboard a Navy vessel, causing a split in C2 processes. In such a case, the COMAFFOR becomes a force provider for the JFACC.

The second node considered within this construct was the AOC (labeled 2 in Figure 3.1).[3] The AOC is responsible for forming the commander's assessment, campaign planning, the production of ATOs, and combat force command execution. The Falconer AOC currently consists of five divisions: Strategy; Plans; Operations; Intelligence, Surveillance, and Reconnaissance; and Air Mobility. The TO-BE AOC organizational structure (see Figure 3.1) differs from the Falconer AOC's *Flight Manual* (2002) by adding a sixth division, Combat Support.[4] AF/IL was exploring this structure as a way to increase attention on ACS issues within the AOC.[5]

The third node assessed was the OSC (labeled 3 in Figure 3.1). The OSC is part of the headquarters staff, usually the NAF associated with the tasked JTF. This node is most commonly referred to simply as "the A-staff."[6] The OSC or the A-staff coordinates with the AOC and is responsible for beddown planning, as well as numerous other support functions. The A-staff should have deep knowledge about the AOR and can assist the AOC in tasks for which that deep knowledge is necessary. While the AOC is responsible for operational planning, the OSC is responsible for maintaining and sustaining assigned forces.

The last node assessed was the MAJCOM theaterwide OSC (labeled 4 in Figure 3.1). This OSC consists of functional area managers who handle resource allocation across the theater. This OSC provides reachback support for the A-staff OSC when necessary, particularly when allocating scarce resources. The OSC and crisis action team (CAT) have generally been organized to meet any immediate needs for a warfighting command that the A-staff or AOC cannot meet, such as options for beddown planning and alternative COAs.

Because of limitations in exercise scope and supporting infrastructure, the assessment team was not able to assess all organizations performing ACS tasks in either exercise.[7] Activities associated with Air Force CCPs and the Air Force CSC nodes did not receive exercise play but were discussed with strategic partners from associated CCPs during teleconferences. Therefore, the functions and relationships of the CCPs and the AF CSC are not analyzed in this report.

---

[3] The AOC depicted here is a Falconer AOC attached to a CAF warfighting headquarters and serving the COMAFFOR. When the COMAFFOR is designated a JFACC, the AOC assigned to him or her transitions to a joint air and space operations center (JAOC). It retains Air Force–unique functions, such as the Air Mobility Division.

[4] Adding a combat support division to the AOC could be a transitional strategy. It would create an opportunity for a senior noncommissioned officer (NCO) and an officer to increase their knowledge about and awareness of combat strategy, planning, and employment. They would be postured to readily assist the three primary process-driven divisions in leveraging CONUS ACS analytic capability as well as on-site ACS staff expertise. After arrival in a TO-BE ACS environment, the division could dissolve into other divisions.

[5] Both exercises included an LRC within the AOC, which served in a similar capacity as a combat support division.

[6] An "A-staff," also referred to as the AFFOR, is organized along the lines of the Joint Staff's "J-staff" and is responsible for warfighting tasks in the Air Force. The designations run A-1 through A-9. See the list of abbreviations for the respective functional areas.

[7] The Expeditionary Wing (E Wing) and the Expeditionary Operations Center (EOC) were not part of the exercises. Both exercises simulated these nodes.

Case Study Findings

TF04 employed all four nodes outlined above (see Figure 3.2). During the exercise, the COMAFFOR was dual-hatted and also served as the JFACC (labeled 1 in Figure 3.2). The COMAFFOR/JFACC and personnel from other MAJCOMs and other services were all afloat, aboard a naval vessel. Because the component commander was not collocated with the AOC or the COMAFFOR staff, two deputy commanders were tasked to lead the COMAFFOR and AOC functional areas.

The AOC (labeled 2 in Figure 3.2) used during this exercise was the PACAF AOC, located adjacent to PACAF Headquarters on Hickam Air Force Base (AFB), Hawaii. The OSC (A-staff) was called the Asia Pacific OSC (APOSC; labeled 3). The APOSC was located at the component NAF (13AF) on Guam, not collocated with the AOC in Hawaii. The MAJCOM theater OSC, called the POSC, was located at PACAF Headquarters on Hickam AFB, across the street from the AOC (labeled 4).

Functional managers worked within their nodes to solve exercise problems, with limited sharing with their functional counterparts at other nodes. All the internode teleconferences were led by the JTF and/or unified commander, who controlled the agenda. Leaders and supervisors within the individual nodes needed a venue in which they could share information and taskings across nodes.

Intranode meetings helped with integration within the nodal functional area. Experience seemed to be a driver toward integration within nodes and across nodes; however, this seemed to depend on established professional relationships and previous work histories. AS-IS thresholds for functional collaboration—even within the same node—seemed rather high.

Between TF04 and AC04, Air Force senior leadership continued to explore options for the new warfighting headquarters construct. Although the construct had not been finalized at the time of this publication, MAJCOMs were making organizational changes, which changed the nodes being observed for this research. This was a significant issue in Europe.

In the European theater, four nodes were exercised during AC04 (see Figure 3.3). The commander of 16AF acted as the COMAFFOR and was dual-hatted as the JFACC (labeled 1 in Figure 3.3). The 16AF staff acted as the OSC A-staff and was called the Operational AFFOR during the exercise (labeled 3).

The USAFE AOC (labeled 2) and the MAJCOM theater OSC, referred to as the Theater AFFOR (labeled 4), were within a new construct called the AFEUR. USAFE is transitioning to become a "warfighting headquarters," a concept the Air Force is adopting in which headquarters and staffs can change from peacetime operations to wartime operations almost immediately. As USAFE makes this transition, the AFEUR, a new organization, has been established as the C2 node for air and space operations in Europe. Figure 3.4 illustrates the current transitional organizational construct. Note that personnel assigned to this new organization for the exercise generally had to create their own roles and exercise play. The AFEUR correlated to what in the past was a staff organization but contained a 24-hour, seven-day-a-week capability similar to that of a C2 node. Note also that the MAJCOM headquarters, USAFE in this

Figure 3.2
Terminal Fury 2004 Organizational Structure

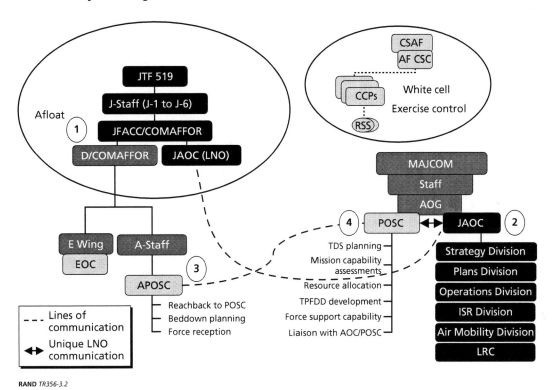

RAND TR356-3.2

Figure 3.3
Austere Challenge 2004 Organizational Structure

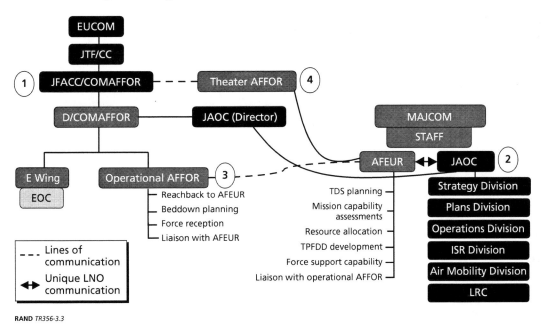

RAND TR356-3.3

Figure 3.4
USAFE March 2004 Interim Organizational Construct

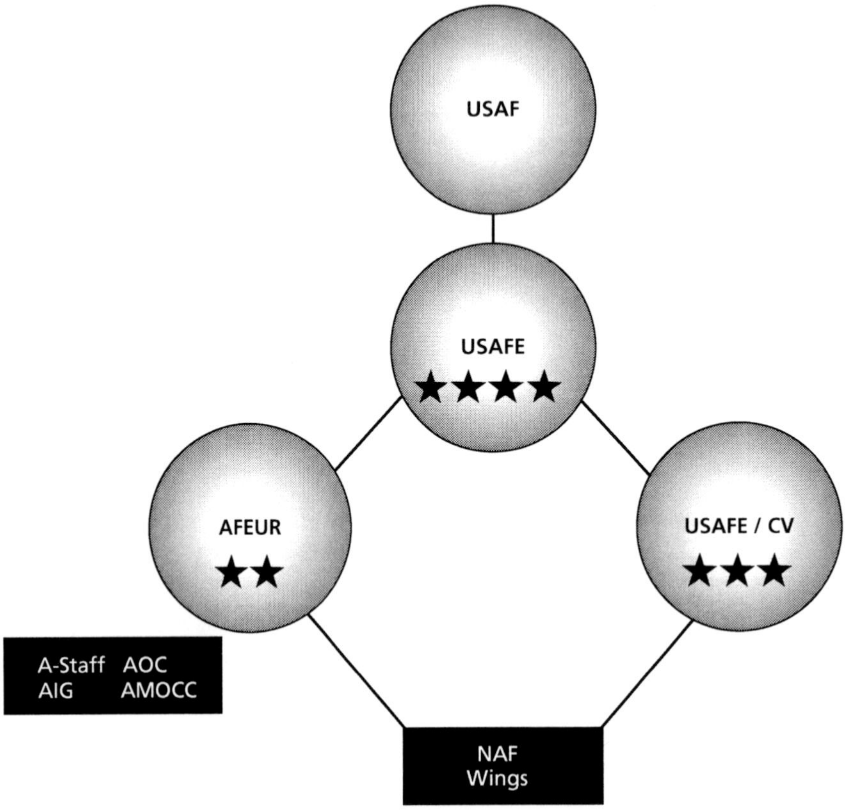

SOURCE: Isherwood (2004), slide 11.
RAND *TR356-3.4*

case, still exists and works "higher-level" issues as a force provider. According to exercise players, both the USAFE staff and the AFEUR would work with a new organization (not depicted in the figure) sited with EUCOM and used to facilitate command-to-command interaction at the theater level. This is important to note because it creates another ACS node for the Air Force, albeit one focused on facilitating unified command interaction with the force provider.

The COMAFFOR/JFACC, the AOC, the Operational AFFOR (16AF), and the Theater AFFOR (AFEUR) were all in different buildings, but all on Ramstein AB, Germany. Physical space limitations required different nodes to occupy different buildings or tent compounds, but the AOC and the Operational AFFOR were collocated in the same complex.

Nodal Organization Implications

Through the assessment process, the assessment teams observed two different organizational constructs, each adapted for theater-specific issues. With the Air Force transitioning to a warfighting headquarters construct, many more organizational constructs may be developed.[8] We found, however, that the particular organizational construct did not affect operations as long as the roles, missions, duties, and responsibilities of each of the C2 nodes were well defined. Clearly defined roles and responsibilities prevent confusion and duplication of effort and allow efficient use of resources. When these roles were in flux or not defined, both current structures were hard pressed to keep up. The TO-BE offers the opportunity for work to be accomplished, shared, and coordinated within nodes and among nodes. For nodes to operate successfully in wartime, roles and responsibilities must be clear in peacetime and practiced in daily effort. Wartime and peacetime systems and procedures should be harmonized.

We also found that physical location did not matter as long as lines of communication were available for use and clear command relationships were defined. Even though units may be split to limit forward footprints, split units work for a common commander within a set chain of command. Assessment teams found that location on site and face-to-face interaction are valuable when the situation is less defined or when lines of communication are less robust.

AOC Staffing and Organization

As previously mentioned, the Falconer AOC's *Flight Manual* (2002) outlines five divisions within the AOC (see Figure 3.1). In addition, the manual outlines a logistics team that works with the Strategy and Plans Divisions on the MAAP team. Various levels of ACS work are outlined in AOC documents,[9] but there is no one specific division for combat support personnel within the AOC. This is expected, since the AOC is a process-organized unit and currently lacking a Combat Support Division. Personnel performing ACS activities in the AOC are supervised by one of the three central core divisions: Strategy, Plans, or Combat Operations. Combat support personnel can be found in the A-staff A-4, a reachback node for the AOC.

Case Study Findings
During TF04, exercise manning provided only a token logistics presence in the AOC, in a group called the LRC. The 502 AOC's concept of operations (CONOPS) detailed a 20-

---

[8] This was not a trivial issue for the ACS community. Some constructs would streamline Air Force management headquarters and set up a single senior commander within each unified command organizational structure. Acting with full COMAFFOR authority, the commander would also become the most eligible to be named as a JFACC. The alternative constructs also tried to limit the number of Falconer AOCs and further focus them on combat operations (primarily as a way to reduce the manpower footprint). In some venues, the COMAFFOR and JFACC were treated and configured as two separate organizations. One consequence of this would be to create a separate and parallel Falconer-like CSC2 weapon system for the COMAFFOR staff, which would increase the fiscal and manpower bills. These constructs also changed the nature of Air Combat Command to that of a "force holder," which would be the primary combat support organization with AFMC.

[9] The Air Force *Air and Space Commander's Handbook for the JFACC* (U.S. Air Force, 2003a) outlines the AOC task flow process and inputs and outputs that integrate logistics and combat support capabilities to define the combat power available for employment. The logistics portion is called the Logistics Specialty Team. USAFE documents also outline a logistics presence in the AOC.

plus manned LRC led by a colonel with a lieutenant colonel deputy. However, the unit type codes (UTCs) used during this exercise had only one logistics-specific personnel requirement. During TF04, there was only one assigned AOC logistics person plus a PACAF Headquarters augmentee, who were then augmented by two temporary duty Air Force Reserve personnel from a reserve component unit based in the U.S. mainland. Because logistics support in the AOC was so limited, combat support–specific tasks were referred back to the A-4 for coordination and worked outside the AOC. AOC-assigned logistics personnel were heavily tasked with manual preparation of PowerPoint slides and error checking of force-level reporting.

Logistics personnel in the AOC were also scarce during some phases of AC04. The Strategy Division had a logistics officer assigned only during the second phase. The division chief and other personnel felt that having logistics personnel in the AOC division provided a needed insight into how best to leverage ACS concerns about basing, sustainment capabilities, and force protection. The MAAP-assigned logistics personnel primarily spent their time manually downloading data and preparing flat files on status (on paper) for the use of the MAAP builders. Some of this was a consequence of problems with the MAAP toolkit that were not solved until later in the exercise.

All AC04 AOC divisions benefited from being collocated with what was referred to as the JFACC staff and sometimes as the forward COMAFFOR staff—the 16AF staff. This group of ACS professionals was well manned with experienced NCOs and officers, who had the advantage of using a NAF CONOPS developed prior to the exercise. Their position was between the combat forces and the remainder of the exercise training audience; so positioned and with an experienced staff, they were able to note problems that were an artifact of the exercise simulation early enough to minimize further exercise complications. They generally acted with confidence and authority. This staff functioned as a separate organization even though reporting to the same general officer as the AOC. As in TF04, issues requiring combat support analysis were referred back to the A-staff for coordination and were worked in the functional area before being shared across nodes.

AOC Staffing Implications

In both theaters, AOC manning was only 50 to 60 percent in the immediate response package. As a result, personnel from the functional staff and the quick response package were used to complete the immediate response package, creating a shortfall for the next level of response (see Figure 3.5).[10] To aid with the manning shortfalls, the AOC currently relies on augmentation from the Air National Guard (in the quick response package) and reserve volunteers. However, Air National Guard personnel may not always be activated or available. The AOC requires adequate staffing to complete the tasks outlined in the Falconer AOC's Flight Manual (2002).

---

[10] The immediate response package should be able to manage 300 sorties per day. The quick response package should be able to manage 500 sorties per day.

Figure 3.5
Sample AOC Manning Levels, FY 2004

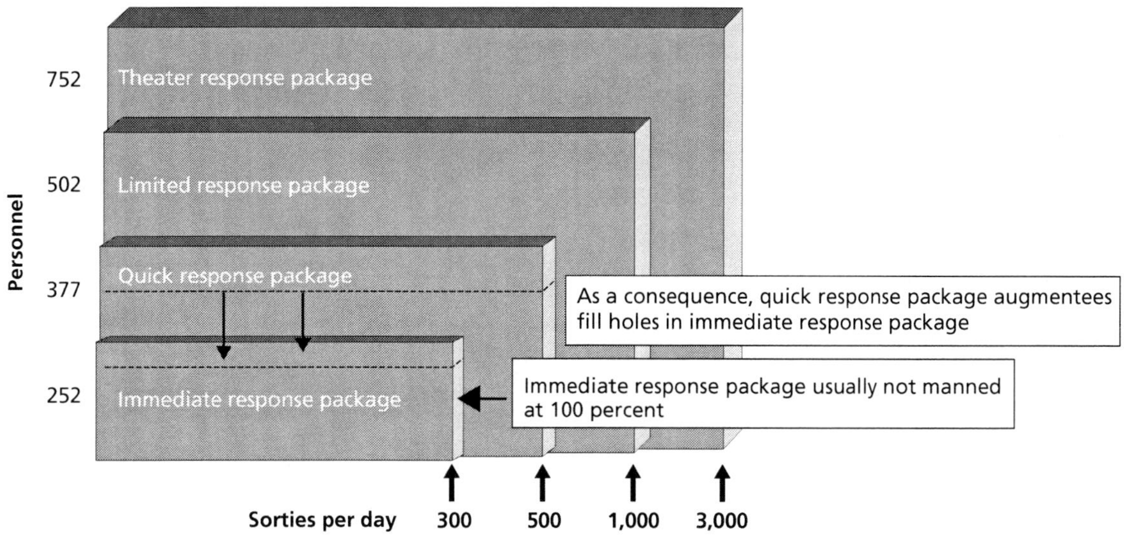

NOTE: Numbers do not include AOC Air Mobility Division augmentation and enablers (200–500 individuals).
RAND TR356-3.5

The logistics personnel manning levels in both AOCs resulted in logisticians focusing on manually entering, manipulating, and verifying data and creating PowerPoint slides or other report information. One result of the scaled-down logistics function in the AOC was that it could not fully represent all ACS functions. Combat support initiatives were referred back to the A-4 for coordination.

When this assessment began, the TO-BE operational architecture, as modified by the Air Force, included a separate division for combat support personnel within the AOC with reach-back to the A-staff to eliminate the parallel C2 issue. This division would be the core logistics capability within the AOC, used to look forward and anticipate combat support issues within the ATO cycle. However, since we completed the assessment, the modified TO-BE structure has changed. A more suitable solution may be to matrix combat support personnel across the five existing divisions in the AOC (see Figure 3.6). This would provide combat support exper-tise in all areas of campaign planning and ATO production without having a separate logistics C2 node, thus integrating combat support planning with the operational campaign planning process.[11]

The presence of logisticians and other ACS functional expertise in the current Falconer AOC is weak, and their role often weaker.[12] If not more logisticians, a more-robust logistics capability in the AOC is certainly needed, whether that expertise be located forward or in CONUS and connected via communications links. The headquarters A-staff should assist the

---

[11] The Air Force ACS CONOPS calls for integrating ACS into operational processes and functions (U.S. Air Force, 1999).

[12] This may be a result of exercise staffing; however, all the MAJCOM staff was battle-rostered into wartime positions, which allotted a very limited number of logistics personnel to the AOC.

Figure 3.6
Revised TO-BE CSC2 Operational Architecture

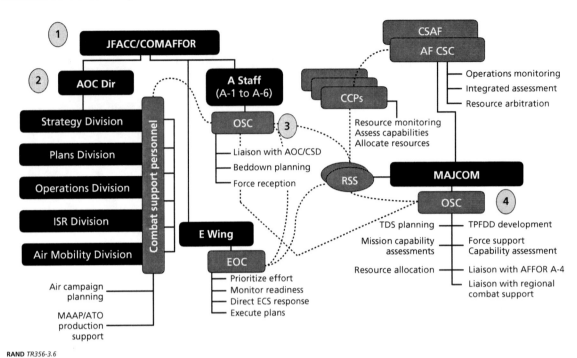

RAND TR356-3.6

AOC in such tasks as beddown planning, which requires deep knowledge. By their nature, some resources, such as fuels and munitions, will receive more attention in the AOC. However, more balance should be achieved across commodities, assessing whether a war plan is supportable or not.

Command and Control Systems Integration and Decision-Support Tools

During both TF04 and AC04, most information was shared using email and telephone. Achieving the full benefit of the CSC2 TO-BE operational architecture will require integrated information systems and products, which are available in a collaborative environment.

Chapter Four discusses the following areas:

- a common operating picture
- exploiting technology.

A Common Operating Picture

A common operating picture is a view of information from several sources integrated into one shared portrayal of data in real or near-real time. This enables leadership and affected personnel access to reliable information so they may make informed decisions. The TO-BE operational architecture relies on the ability of personnel at each node to assess and query common data sets with confidence that the data are "good." Personnel may have the same data, but each individual's view of the data will be task- and/or position-dependent.

Case Study Findings

During TF04, the assessment team observed an ad hoc mix of systems; the same was true during AC04. Systems differed not only across nodes but sometimes within an individual node. The A-staff during TF04 used one civil engineering software package, while the theater OSC (the A-staff's reachback counterpart) used a different system. Two different nodes used two different systems with two different data sets to answer the same question.

Each functional area within combat support uses different systems (hardware, software, and data processes). Some data overlapped, but each system had a different function and provided unique data depending on the specific situation and initial information available. Each MAJCOM has theater-specific software, which added to the data complexity.

During AC04, an information management (IM) plan (USAFE, 2004a), referred to as the *in-flight guide*, was created as a first step toward developing a common operating picture. This relatively simple step provided personnel with a stable organization structure in which they could quickly distinguish between current and draft information products, as well as providing a place to find the necessary information reliably. The plan was first used in the AOC and the A-staff. It was later expanded to include the theater OSC. An AC04 portal and electronic work structure were also established. Daily presentations were archived on the AOC's server and so could be referred to later.

Common Operating Picture Implications

Communications capabilities in the A-staff (less so in the AOC operational areas) are currently one-to-one systems and work processes. Manual processes are used for updating data and providing support to the AOC.[1] The common operating picture for the ACS system, as observed during TF04 and AC04, was a simple PowerPoint presentation that provided a daily logistics snapshot for the warfighter. Changing the technology used to complete work tasks will be a major part of moving to the TO-BE common operating picture.

A first step would be to define what data are necessary for each CSC2 node. Currently, there is duplication of information. Perhaps one software system could be used to generate more of the necessary data. A common system architecture (a data repository with shared software) should be established for all nodes. Having all nodes operate on software systems that can leverage open-standards data and information would provide a common environment for work processes, the first step toward a common operating picture. Personnel need the capability to create TO-BE formats that reach into dynamic databases maintained by the data owner at each level and present the information in a manner that tees up ACS decisions for a decisionmaker. The display format must make sense to the people working at each node within the context of that work and the decisions they support.

Providing a deliberate IM plan and organization for information on the servers would be another step toward developing a common operating picture. This does not require additional technology, only a consensus for how material will be stored and accessed by the nodes within the Air Force. The development of a deliberate process for IM, such as the in-flight guide used during AC04, would alleviate some of these issues. In fact, as AC04 moved to completion, the IM and Operational Employment Divisions in the AOC were in the process of creating such a plan. More than any other initiative, the effect on clarifying internodal communications and coordination requirements within and outside the AOC was fairly dramatic.[2]

In the future, forward operating locations may be constrained by force protection, host nation, or other factors so that there may not be sufficient AOC and A-staff personnel in the forward area to accomplish the range of ACS or employment taskings. A common operating picture with a common system architecture and a deliberate IM plan would allow taskings to be accomplished via reachback with little additional technological effort.

---

[1] During the period of the research, an automated process for developing the MAAP was under development that would reduce the number of operational AFSC personnel in the MAAP Cell (Combat Plans Division) by approximately half. Very little was being done to take advantage of these TO-BE capabilities to accomplish ACS tasks.

[2] Discussions and observations with 32 Air Operations Group IM and Operations Employment Division personnel at Ramstein AB, March 2004. Additional discussion concerning effect of change, with WPC White Cell personnel roleplaying JFC staff and U.S. European Command J-4 personnel, Einsedlerhof Air Station, March 2004.

Exploiting Technology

Currently, there is little or no machine-to-machine reporting for ACS tasks. PowerPoint slides are built manually using data from force-level message traffic or telephone calls. Generally, slides are recreated at each node using node-specific briefing formats, which could be reduced or eliminated with machine-to-machine interfaces.

There are some fairly advanced collaborative tools in the AS-IS Falconer AOC, working with common data sets available to personnel within the AOC. However, even in the AOC, very few collaborative tools have been applied to ACS tasks.[3] Because of the desire to continue to reduce AOC manning, some fairly sophisticated data mining and transfer tools have been created to build specific AOC products, such as the MAAP.

As we noted, more progress could be made toward the TO-BE architecture if work processes and node procedures for gathering and storing information could be put into place. This could require leveraging the current level of technology with appropriate changes to ACS doctrine and training programs. We noted during AC04 that preparing people was significant in creating a TO-BE work environment. It may be that preparing people and building expectations for TO-BE communications between nodes creates an internal demand for using available technology in a more TO-BE manner, resulting in gains in quality and timeliness of information.

Case Study Findings

During both TF04 and AC04, almost all communications between nodes were point-to-point communications using secure (for example, secure telephone unit [STU] III or Secure Internet Protocol Router Network [SIPRNET]) or nonsecure (for example, unclassified telephones or the Nonsecure Internet Protocol Router Network [NIPRNET] email) lines of communication—all one to one.[4]

In an effort to move from point-to-point communications to a more collaborative environment, one of the exercise initiatives during TF04 was the use of collaborative tools, such as Information Workspace (IWS) and Collaboration at Sea (CAS). The COMAFFOR/JFACC and the A-staff nodes used IWS; however, there were some exercise communications limitations that constrained connectivity between the nodes. The COMAFFOR/JFACC node suc-

---

[3] During the Air Force Joint Experimentation spiral development process for FY 2000, several ACS-focused tools were evaluated. Some of these have made it into ACS-tasked organizations (for example, tools to help organize and transmit information on potential force beddown sites). TF04 and AC04 observations indicate that not enough of the technology or the new work processes have made it to the field to have an effect on ACS capabilities. We have noted that ACS is listed as a Key Investment Category for the Air Force but have observed very little progress in getting the technology into the field.

[4] The team noted that, even when the communication was many to one, as would be the case when the information was transmitted in a formatted message, the feedback and fact-checking remained one to one. During the exercises, we noted several instances in which the commander's trust and confidence in ACS personnel was questioned because of data that were either out of context, did not match other compiled sets, or lacked a day-and-time signature (sometimes as important as the data). One munitions issue took two AOC munitions personnel one shift to sort out and delayed work on the MAAP for that day. The "fix" resulted in a series of PowerPoint slides being added to the JFACC daily briefing with the associated heavy manual workload to create and maintain the slide data. All this could have been prevented by a relational database using a format to gather data from unit reporting.

cessfully used CAS to post task lists, briefings, and the event log. The other nodes did not use CAS during the exercise.

We did not observe collaborative tools in any of the nodes during AC04. The only automated system we saw was in A-1, which automatically updated personnel information from the Joint Operations Planning and Execution System (JOPES). By the end of AC04, Web sites were being used. Only the A-3 personnel in the theater OSC who used JOPES had a newsgroup for sharing data. The AOC Time Critical Targeting cell was using some chat capabilities. The A-staff did not have direct access to any combat support information systems, such as Core Automated Maintenance System (CAMS), CAS, or the Fuels Automated System, greatly limiting its ability to build or access a common collaborative data system for unit-level data.

Exploiting Technology Implications

One-to-one interaction without common data and automatic report generation leads to reporting of facts and figures rather than capabilities. Manually entering data is time consuming and can result in errors. Manually creating slides with bits of information on them, as seen throughout both of these exercises, illustrates a focus on data as opposed to a warfighting capability. Moving to a computer-to-computer interface would allow individuals more time to analyze capabilities instead of creating data slides.

A mission application, such as the MAAP Tool Kit, bundles together program applications that automatically build worksheets and transfer information into other applications. The MAAP Tool Kit could be used today to sort through large data sets, such as personnel, fuels, or munitions tracking data. More systems with similar capabilities are needed in the combat support area. The information and data ACS activities use is ripe for information technology, such as using Really Simple Syndication (RSS) and extensible markup language (XML) to format data. XML has been used in recent U.S. Joint Forces Command exercises, in which it provided situational awareness for decisionmakers, leading to quicker command decisions (Colaizzi, 2005).

Anything that can be broken down into discrete data and text can be distributed via RSS technology. RSS feeds can be used most effectively to update ongoing work and processes and can display the information that is new. Just as a Web-enabled chat capability has improved military intelligence and such operational processes as time-sensitive targeting, RSS-aware programs can subscribe to feeds that report on force-level status changes or inventories. IWS can also be an effective tool; however, in TF04, not all the exercise participants had access to or were trained to use it. In moving to the TO-BE architecture, it will be necessary to develop a collaborative strategy that will allow not just the AOC and A-staff nodes but all Air Force combat support to interact. The air mobility and intelligence communities are engaged in developing strategies for their own functional areas; perhaps some of these collaborative and distributed work approaches can be leveraged for ACS operational-level warfighter tasks.

A similar technology capability development could help in two areas. First, personnel focused on ACS tasks need better means of creating the data at the owners' location and sharing it between nodes, using formats that help each node monitor and assess the state of ACS activities. Second, the senior warfighter staff and CSC2 personnel need to gain visibility over who is doing ACS work so that they can leverage personnel and parallel processes across combat support nodes. They can then look for deep knowledge over ACS issues that affect combat power, similar to what happens in the intelligence and targeting communities. Without visibility into the tasking and completion of ACS off-site work, ACS personnel will be hard pressed to maintain the trust and confidence of their COMAFFOR; JFACC; or, ultimately, the JFC commander. This technology already exists in systems, such as the MAAP Tool Kit and IWS; it just needs to be adapted for ACS use in the warfighter context.

CHAPTER FIVE

Training and Education

Exercises play a large role in training and educating Air Force personnel. They enable teams to work together, and personnel learn by *doing*, building on more-traditional education and training. At the operational level, warfighting headquarters exercises allow individual functional teams to gain work experience in their own nodes as well as across nodes. One aspect of this type of training is that scenarios can be built to evaluate new war plans or organizational constructs. For both TF04 and AC04, planners sought to gain more-complete knowledge of contingency plans and how organizations worked together under stress and to test organizational constructs. The exercises in these case studies were offered by the participating Air Force MAJCOM as candidate operational-level environments in which ACS activities would be played out under a joint warfighting scenario.[1] In addition, assessment teams discussed the exercise and training program with operations and logistics personnel in both affected headquarters. One aspect of this discussion was how best to involve nontheater nodes in theater exercise play.

The baseline exercise training opportunity at the operational level is the Blue Flag series of exercises that are conducted for each NAF commander and staff. While personnel from other services and national agencies may participate, Blue Flag training audiences are limited to the personnel within each NAF and supporting below-the-line organizations, such as intelligence and operations groups. Theater exercises, such as TF04 and AC04, allow the affected operational-level personnel to work with other service components and combatant command C2 capabilities. According to personnel at both USAFE and PACAF, both the Blue Flag and theater C2 exercises are valuable. While some participants may be from supporting combatant commands, such as U.S. Strategic Command and U.S. Transportation Command, CONUS-based combat support forces generally do not play.

With the Air Force evolving to more of an expeditionary approach to providing forces and ACS business practices that place more capability in the rear, there is little opportunity to

---

[1] Both exercises were sponsored by the theater combatant command. TF04 created a very large training audience that included command personnel from the unified command and all its senior service components. While it occurred in a broad joint context, AC04's training audience was primarily the new theaterwide AFFOR, what was essentially 16AF staff, and the USAFE AOC led by the 32 AOG. COMUSAFE had much greater latitude in designing AC04, but TF04 created a richer and more dynamic joint training environment, with simulation and role players only at the national and force levels. For both exercises, a large part of the ACS activity preparing for war was assumed to have occurred prior to the exercise time frame. AC04 did phase in ACS play in phases I and II because of the need to create the exercise database for force beddown.

involve personnel from the full range of CSC2 nodes in exercise play. As a consequence, personnel in the forward area are developing procedures and practices without input from and the participation of other ASC nodes, such as AMC and the Air Force Combat Support Center. They actually work together only during real wartime deployments and crisis responses. Personnel in the forward area do not make demands on CONUS support capabilities until there is a real crisis. With more ACS capability moving out of the Air Force warfighting headquarters, there needs to be a deliberate effort to involve nontheater CSC2 nodes in regular operational-level training exercises.

Assessment team members noted that current exercise designs do not fully support expeditionary combat support training objectives. Often, logistics issues are disregarded in exercise play because of the inability to simulate strategic air and surface deployment, logistics in-transit visibility, sustainment requirements, and the replication of organizations not participating in the training audience (for example, AMC, AFMC, the U.S. Transportation Command, and the AF CSC). Logistics issues, including allocation of scarce resources, rely on coordination between many nodes; often, many of these other nodes do not participate in the exercise, so their input is either scripted by exercise role players or completely left out.

Exercise play for both TF04 and AC04 incorporated logistics issues, and much was learned from the ACS involvement. During TF04, PACOM joint and Air Force logistics personnel were part of the exercise planning effort and were included in planning conferences and scenario design. However, many ACS activities were scripted, not requiring real ACS effort.

Much of the focus during AC04 was on the training and education of the new AFEUR staff and the theater OSC. One aspect was to explore the working relationship between the JTF component commander, his AOC and staff, and the theaterwide COMAFFOR capability being tested. The other supporting ACS nodes, located in CONUS, were not as engaged in the exercise. Air Force personnel based in CONUS or providing rear-based theater support should become more assertive in working with warfighter C2 nodes and forces. Supervisors and commanders should look for opportunities to participate in their appropriate roles in theater-led exercises and training venues.

During both exercises, assessment team personnel talked with CONUS ACS nodes during the end-of-day teleconference with the strategic partners. In some cases, CONUS-based personnel took issues and problems from the exercise to work offline and report back the next day to exercise assessment teams. While these individuals were not directly involved in the two exercises, this level of involvement increased their awareness of theater ACS challenges and provided them with a set of "homework" problems they could work within their organizations during the exercise period. This is an example of how the training opportunity presented in a theater-controlled exercise could be leveraged for training node personnel. This low-risk interaction provides an opportunity to better understand and establish the warfighter demand on Air Force combat support capabilities. It also provides the warfighter ACS personnel with a deeper and more functional look at ACS options provided in the course of the exercise play. It is a method of allowing tacit information to become more visible to ACS professionals as they engage in warfighter-based activity. As information becomes more explicit across nodes, a broader consensus on actionable alternatives is possible.

Implications

Exercises need to be designed to complete the education and training process, providing all personnel a full opportunity to practice and learn by *doing*. Technology will only be able to go so far into the TO-BE vision; personnel will have to develop new work processes that help leverage the limited manpower available and their professional capabilities. Much of their tasking in the AS-IS CSC2 structure seems to be manual data entry and fact-checking, which does not fully employ ACS personnel's functional expertise and knowledge. In the TO-BE architecture, it will be necessary to create the ability to do discrete tasks and share information across CSC2 nodes. The architecture must also provide personnel the ability to look within the Air Force combat support structure for key knowledge and capabilities that will open up more combat power for a given set of resources.

The Air Force logistics community needs a venue (physical or virtual) in which to build experience across nodes. The Joint National Training Capability,[2] with live, virtual, and constructive training, may be one way to fulfill training requirements. Another way may be to use formal classroom education with well-planned scenarios and desired learning outcomes to help in building expertise. Today, the only demand on CONUS-based combat support comes during a crisis. Personnel, unless they have direct theater experience, can only guess as they anticipate the problems theater ACS personnel face. To fully achieve the TO-BE architecture, it will be important to build experience and train all ACS nodes. As mentioned previously, ACS personnel need to develop a history of experience in supporting the warfighter. This is necessary to build an acceptable level of warfighter trust and confidence. Without a way to gain this history outside of a crisis, capabilities not based in the theater will always be suspect until called on—and then must prove themselves under the stress of a contingency operation. People and organizations do not fully understand the operational demands until they experience them and work under them for a sustained period. The Red Flag series of exercises was created to give operational forces the peacetime equivalent of ten wartime sorties, and the ACS community needs the same opportunity. A modeling and simulation capability to project future requirements would be beneficial in enabling proactive, rather than reactive, combat support.

The TO-BE architecture needs personnel who are used to working in a collaborative environment in which information is entered by data owners and used across all the nodes. This requires systems that utilize machine-to-machine reporting and exhibit some automation in rolling up data into information displays for the user. The TO-BE tries to place the logistics specialist at an information vantage point from which he can gain knowledge over the operational environment, the commander's intent, and combat support potential to provide pre-

---

[2] U.S. Joint Forces Command's Joint National Training Capability is not expected to be fully mission capable until 2009.

cisely defined combat capabilities.[3] Combat support education will require more training experiences that involve the appropriate staff and C2 nodes (such as the AOC) working together to build experience and to pattern work processes. To fully realize the potential for the TO-BE, the entire Air Force ACS community (AFMC, AMC, etc.) needs to be involved in an exercise like TF04 or AC04.

Educational and training programs should be sensitive to balancing deep knowledge with a broad understanding of warfighting processes and capabilities. Deep functional knowledge will still be useful, and career paths need to provide opportunities to gain experience with ACS forces and technical support activities. Personnel in the forward area will need the ability to leverage this capability for the warfighter and better integrate ACS operational-level activities into information optimized for operations planning and employment. With fewer personnel based in the forward area, it will also be necessary to train CONUS-based personnel through participation in theater exercises.

ACS activities also need to invest in people who know how to handle information and build databases. Operations capabilities in the AOC have been fueled by access to personnel who understand the power of relational databases and information display. Information in the ACS realm should be displayed in ways that tee up decisions for functional managers and present the consequences for the combat force of the options offered.

Providing ACS professionals (senior NCOs, civilians, and officers) with educational tools and training venues should enhance CSC2 abilities. The Air Force must invest not just in technology in moving to the TO-BE but also in education and training opportunities for ACS-engaged personnel. This effect will help fine-tune future doctrine and prepare operations planners for proactive ACS information that can help shape and define the combat power available.

---

[3] It is interesting to note that this can be realized using a relatively low level of technology. During Joint Expeditionary Force Experiment 2000, ACS personnel working with some TO-BE tools and in an information-managed decision environment were able to turn within the ATO planning and employment time lines to provide a set of options for the ATO planners. In addition, one civil engineer–oriented tool was used to provide a weapons of mass destruction target analysis earlier than one offered by the traditional intelligence-only path. While the target solution in that case was the same, it arrived earlier and with deeper analysis, building greater trust and confidence in command capabilities. (Joint Expeditionary Force Experiment 2000 observations and discussions with ACS and IM personnel.)

CHAPTER SIX

Summary Observations

Implementing the TO-BE architecture Air Force–wide could standardize C2 for combat support activities. Investing in ACS and IM education, as well as in some collaborative work strategies and tools, could improve communications across Air Force ACS nodes. From the exercise observations, it appears that the primary advantage to the Air Force in moving from AS-IS manual processes to the TO-BE will be in gaining the professional expertise and tacit knowledge from its personnel. Currently, manual processes place a high demand on keyboard entry, fact-checking, and parallel reporting. TO-BE work processes and systems should free the ACS professional to apply his or her knowledge to warfighter problems, anticipate consequences, and help shape the combat force capability.

Assessment team members were sensitive to the fact that the drive to establish an ACS CONOPS and achieve the TO-BE architecture is not primarily a consequence of a dramatic failure of the AS-IS capability. As noted in the literature of transformation and innovation in organizations, there seems to be ample evidence that, when performance fails to meet expectations, organizations search for new ways of doing work. Likewise, there is evidence that some change is driven less by problems than by solutions, for example, new technology (March, 1988, p. 174). Assessment team members noted that neither seemed to be the primary driver in this case; instead, they found that the primary drive to change was motivated, first, by a realization of just how critical ACS activities are to defining the combat force; second, by changes in the service combat support community's role as a "holder of force capability" for the combatant commands' employment; and, finally, by internal and external constraints on ACS manpower now coupled with a potential erosion of expert knowledge associated with the loss of experienced leaders.[1] Assessment teams noted that both the top leadership level and the professional workforce echoed these motivations for change. The new technology and the fiscal opportunity presented in the current reorganization of employment-focused C2 systems makes a move toward a CSC2 TO-BE possible now. This situation presents ACS leadership with the opportunity to avoid a dramatic failure in the future.

Following subsections summarize the observations the assessment teams made during their exercise experiences.

---

[1] One trump card for ACS execution has long been its use of experienced senior NCOs and relatively low-cost enlisted manpower in the functional stovepipes.

Organizational Structure

Differing organizational constructs exist today. Some of these may be fine-tuned for different operational environments. As long as the roles and responsibilities are well defined, the organizational structure should not have a large influence:

- Air Force CSC2 nodes should fully understand their roles and authority when working with warfighting headquarters.
- Warfighting headquarters should learn—through common practice—the value of Air Force service-led support.
- All organizations should share information with appropriate CSC2 nodes.
- Within the theater, each organizational node should understand and execute its responsibilities within the tasked operational authority. (Theaterwide capabilities must work to enable CSC2 capabilities assigned to a JTC with specific joint tasks to perform.)

We suggest that a logistics component could be matrixed across AOC divisions to provide combat support expertise and eliminate a parallel C2 structure in the warfighting headquarters staff.

C2 Systems Integration and Decision-Support Tools

A common IM architecture could be defined so all nodes are working from common information:

- An IM plan could be developed for managing the common system architecture so that a common operating picture can be developed.
- ACS systems and processes should be integrated with operational systems at the data level.

Technology should be exploited to allow sharing of information through Web-based tools; RSS-enabled data and text streams; and automatic, rather than manual, data builds for decisionmaker viewing. Using technology to share common data should allow more time for "what if" analysis and resource allocation, and less time will be spent building PowerPoint slides.

Training and Education

Exercises should be designed to engage all nodes in the ACS arena:

- Provide an opportunity to work across nodes in a collaborative environment.
- Construct Blue Flag exercises to engage ACS personnel.
- Develop a strategy to involve key CONUS CSC2 nodes in theater C2 exercises.

- Continue to manage functional career areas to acquire the deep knowledge necessary to perform at the level of precision needed for fielding and sustaining combat forces, developing
  - an appreciation of operational risk as it applies to providing forces
  - fluency with modeling and simulation of ACS activity to better influence operational outcomes to meet desired effects during force structure beddown and planning.
- Build the means for gaining knowledge of best practices across ACS for the entire Air Force.
- Teach ACS critical thinking and problem solving in an operational environment.
- Invest in the education of personnel who understand ACS functional areas so that they can learn how to best leverage technology and TO-BE IM processes.

Terminal Fury 2004 Case Study

As the Air Force was beginning its transition to the TO-BE operational architecture, the AF/ILG was tasked to assess the implementation. Terminal Fury 2004 (TF04), a PACOM exercise held in December 2003, provided an opportunity to observe the TO-BE vision at important CSC2 nodes in an operational environment. An annual C2 exercise, Terminal Fury was designed to exercise a PACOM operational plan or a potential COA. The assessment team used TF04 to observe the CSC2 nodes and information flows in the TO-BE operational architecture and to explore and build knowledge of their integrated combat support systems and processes. TF04 provided an operational environment that allowed observation of the combat support structure under stress. Using exercise topics as a focus, the assessment team reviewed how information flowed between and within nodes, what systems were used, and how personnel involved in the topic of focus were trained. The CSC2 assessment team did not change the exercise scenario or alter PACOM and PACAF exercise goals. The exercise provided a unique opportunity to observe a range of CSC2 nodes involved in executing the scenario, such as a JTF headquarters staff, a COMAFFOR/JFACC, an AFFOR staff (the engaged NAF, 13AF, with elements afloat and in garrison), the AOC (including afloat and rear elements tasked to support the JFACC[1]), and MAJCOM theater reachback (POSC).

The assessment of the CSC2 operational architecture during TF04 was successful. While there are issues that should be addressed in moving to the TO-BE vision, personnel are the reason the CSC2 system worked during TF04.

TF04 was a PACOM command post exercise, not a field exercise. Organizations above or outside the PACOM AOR and forces below the operational level did not participate. The training audience consisted of the exercise PACOM staff; standing JTF 519's commander and staff; PACAF service components and their C2 nodes; and the JTF land, sea, and air component staffs that were created for the exercise. Because of this level of participation, inputs above and below the theater and force levels were simulated; certain functions were not performed; and/or scripted responses were given to queries. Other issues, such as reporting inconsistencies, resulted from the exercise's artificiality. When the exercise environment itself was responsible for a problem or concern, it is noted in this report.

TF04, as a PACOM exercise, was limited to the scenario as PACOM scripted it. The scenario created some organizational challenges that may not apply in other theaters. No changes

---

[1] During TF04, the AOC was not physically collocated with the JFACC.

were made to the exercise for the sake of this assessment. However, the CSC2 assessment team did select a few of the operational challenges and issues that arose during TF04 for discussion with the Air Force CSC2 strategic partners, who participated in a daily teleconference.[2] These tabletop exercises helped facilitate discussion between the assessment team and strategic partners. Some strategic partners addressed these issues with their own staffs and reported back anticipated COAs as if they had been active players.

Organizational Structure

The AF/IL CSC2 TO-BE architecture provides an organizational construct to ensure C2 functions are performed through a standard or uniform arrangement of personnel, equipment, communications, facilities, and procedures throughout the Air Force. Figure A.1 illustrates the current understanding of nodes in the TO-BE CSC2 operational architecture. The CSC2 construct that the COMAFFOR employs enables planning, directing, coordinating, and controlling forces and combat support operations in its role as a service component to the JFC. It is recognized, though not obvious in the figure, that both the AOC and the A-staff perform ACS tasks.[3]

Observations

The objectives of the assessment team were to observe how the CSC2 TO-BE organizational construct should be employed and to assess its effectiveness. Because of limitations in TF04 exercise design, the assessment team was not able to assess all organizations performing ACS tasks. The primary focus of the assessment team's observation was on how the TF04 JTF COMAFFOR OSC (the APOSC) interacted with the JFACC AOC and how they interacted with the HQ PACAF's theaterwide capability, the POSC.[4] Activities associated with Air Force commodity control points and the AF CSC nodes did not receive any exercise play during TF04 but were discussed during the assessment team's daily teleconferences. These nodes and their interplay with theater CSC2 nodes will be assessed in future case studies.

Our observations fall into the following areas:

- nodal organizations afloat
- A-4 and A-7 responsibilities
- AOC location and staffing.

---

[2] The CSC2 strategic partners were USAFE, AFMC, AMC, and the AFC2ISRC.

[3] Several documents outline the various levels of ACS work in the AOC. The Falconer AOC's *Flight Manual* details a logistics team that works with the Strategy Division and the MAAP Cell within the Plans Division. The PACAF AOC CONOPS outlines a robust logistics team manned by personnel from all logistics functional specialties and led by a colonel with a lieutenant colonel as deputy.

[4] The TF04 exercise design did create a level of complexity in command relationships that does not exist outside the TF04 experience. The JTF COMAFFOR and JFACC were the same person, just as doctrine suggests. However, because the component commander was not collocated with the AOC or the COMAFFOR staff (he was aboard a naval vessel, with the JTF commander and other component commanders), two deputy commanders were tasked to lead the COMAFFOR and JFACC-AOC functional areas. HQ PACAF remained in the role of theater component to PACOM, with primary responsibility for forces and support tasks outside the joint operating area (JOA).

Figure A.1
TO-BE CSC2 Organizational Structure

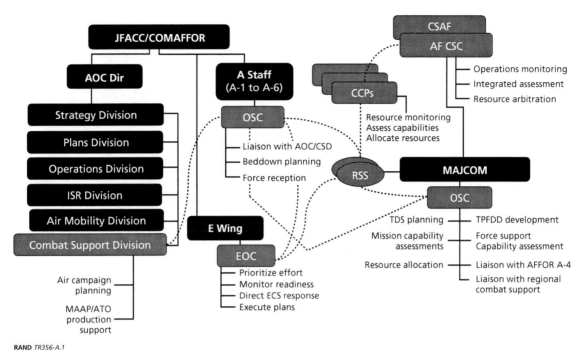

RAND *TR356-A.1*

Nodal Organizations Afloat. The main C2 elements (forward) employed during this exercise were afloat on a naval vessel. The JTF commander, the COMAFFOR/JFACC, deputy COMAFFOR/deputy JFACC, the joint force maritime component commander, and their staffs, along with representatives from Special Operations Forces and space representation from U.S. Strategic Command, were all located forward or afloat (see Figure A.2). The PACAF AOC is not collocated with the APOSC, which is located with the component NAF staff on Guam (13AF); it is physically adjacent to the POSC and PACAF Headquarters on Hickam AFB, Hawaii. The commander of USPACOM and the JTF commander appointed the Eleventh Air Force commander (11AF/CC) (Alaska) to be the JFACC instead of the Thirteenth Air Force commander (13 AF/CC) (Guam), as outlined in doctrine given the location of forces and the exercise JOA.[5] The exercise JOA was predominately in the 13AF AOR. The JFACC—instead of the 13AF/CC (Guam), as doctrine would ordinarily have indicated, given the location—acted as the deputy COMAFFOR and the 13AF staff as the COMAFFOR staff. The COMAFFOR CSC2 node on Guam was as the APOSC.

While some organizational structures and reporting chains were established and specifically detailed prior to the execution of the exercise, others were not addressed. In PACAF, the PACAF director of operations leads the deliberate planning process, coordinating work across the staff and with the joint staff at PACOM and other service components to create a plan

---

[5] Air Force Doctrine Document 2, *Organization and Employment of Aerospace Power* (USAF, 1998) recommends naming the commander with the predominance of air forces the JFACC.

Figure A.2
Terminal Fury 2004 Organizational Structure

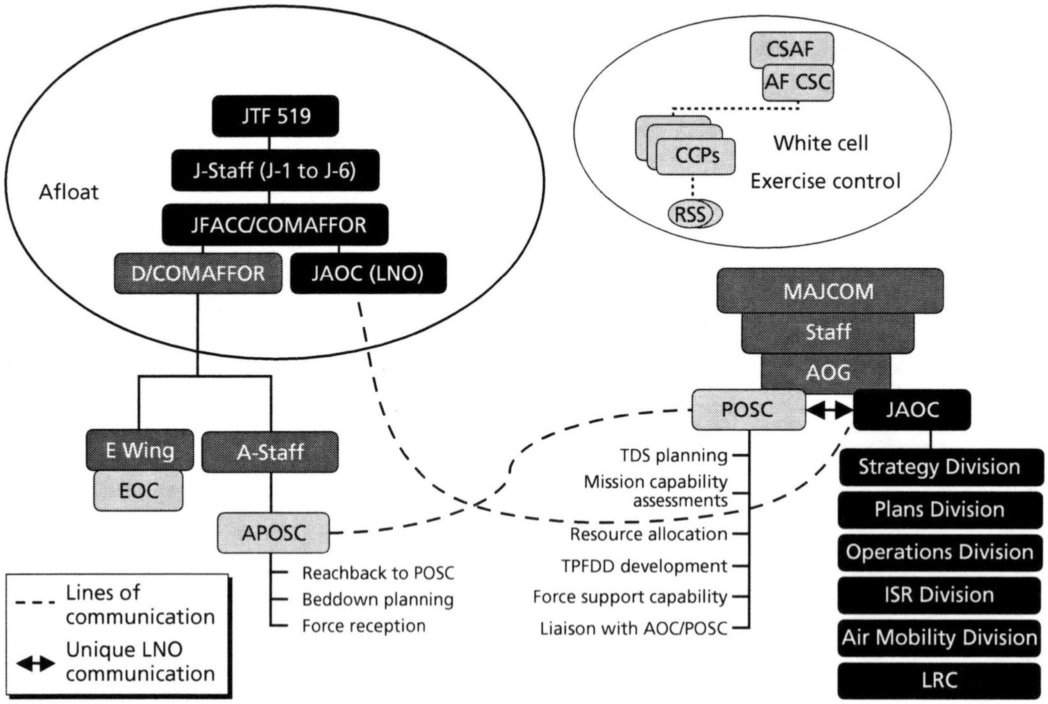

RAND *TR356-A.2*

that meets the mission requirements. The Eleventh Air Expeditionary Task Force draft operations order (2003) detailed C2 from the joint perspective. The AFFOR Command and Control CONOPS (Deputy Chief of Staff, Air and Space Operations, 2002) discussed C2 from the COMAFFOR and the AOC perspective. The CONOPS for the POSC and the PACAF Contingency Action Team (502nd Air Operations Squadron, 2002) discussed how the Commander, Pacific Air Force (COMPACAF) C2 organization (POSC) operates and interfaces with both PACOM and the 56th Air and Space Operations Squadron's AOC. The *Air and Space Commander's Handbook for the JFACC* (U.S. Air Force, 2003a) provides specific details on how the AOC will operate and interface with other organizations, from both the Air Force and joint perspectives. The Eleventh Air Expeditionary Task Force Terminal Fury 2004 draft operations order clearly defined the 13AF APOSC as the central point to collect all COMAFFOR information and requirements. Not formally addressed were reporting chains between the APOSC and the POSC or how the POSC would interact with the JFACC or AOC. The physical location of the AOC and the POSC affected the information flows within the above structure. These two organizations were across the street from each other on Hickam AFB. Within the POSC, there was no clear definition of the roles and responsibilities of the A-staff, for example, how the A-4 and the A-7 should work beddown planning issues.

A-4 and A-7 Responsibilities. During TF04, the issue of bedding down forces and aircraft began as a consequence of exercise play. The issue centered on relocating aircraft from their planned beddown location. During the 2200Z teleconference on December 7, the PACOM vice commander tasked the PACAF/CC to work the issue in the POSC. At the same time, the COMAFFOR had the deputy COMAFFOR task his staff in the APOSC to work the same issue. The APOSC knew the POSC was also working a beddown issue, but did not communicate or coordinate with the POSC director regarding the tasking. Similarly, there was limited or no observed communication between the POSC and the APOSC. The contingency planning team (CPT), a theater-level organization within the 502 AOG on Hickam AFB continued to work the beddown issue with all required functional area experts even after the APOSC had officially responded to the task.

The CPT is responsible for developing possible responses to a contingency and for refining the plan following the selection of a COA (PACAF, 2002). The team consists of applicable functional experts from the supporting POSC A-staff and can be augmented with other headquarters staff functional experts as required. All functional representatives are initially included; each individual area then determines its own level of participation, depending on the scenario. During peacetime, the CPT examines possible contingency scenarios in theater and prepares COAs. However, if a JTF is activated for a war or crisis, the JTF COMAFFOR has primary responsibility for air COA development within the JTF AOR. In that case, the PACAF CPT should provide reachback assistance only on request.

The CPT is structured to allow flexibility based on the individual situation. For example, during the TF04 beddown planning process, personnel from the POSC worked with the AOC Strategy Division. The A-7 representative, a civil engineer, assumed coleadership of the CPT. More commonly, the Logistics Readiness functional area (A-4) is the lead for facilitating beddown planning (U.S. Air Force, 2001; U.S. Air Force, 2003b).

In the POSC, A-7 was a newly designated cell and was not addressed in the current PACAF CONOPs. The division of duties and responsibilities between A-4 and A-7 was confusing to the assessment team, which asked for clarification. The functional area representatives explained the situation by saying that A-7 was responsible for base operating support.[6] Further discussion led to a division of responsibility within the beddown planning process and contingency reporting based on commodity and infrastructure. For example, A-4 reported on the quantities of fuel and fuel mobility support equipment, while A-7 reported on the status of fuel storage facilities, hydrant systems, etc. The POSC CONOPS (PACAF, 2002) says civil engineers are the focal point for "installations support for beddown and support of deploying units."

AOC Location and Staffing. The principal NAF headquarters for TF04, 13AF, does not have an AOC assigned; therefore, the PACAF AOC, on Hickam AFB, was tasked with supporting the JTF 519 JFACC/COMAFFOR. The 13AF APOSC (Andersen AFB, Guam) supported the COMAFFOR staff, which was on Guam. Supporting organizations, such as the PACAF POSC, were referred to as *rear* elements, even though their serving commands were not physically divided into forward and rear locations. Figure A.3 illustrates the AOC's organization for the exercise.

---

[6] While the functional area representatives were not confused or concerned, this did not resolve the discussion because there is no universal definition, either in the joint community or within the Air Force, for base operating support.

Figure A.3
Terminal Fury 2004 AOC Organizational Structure

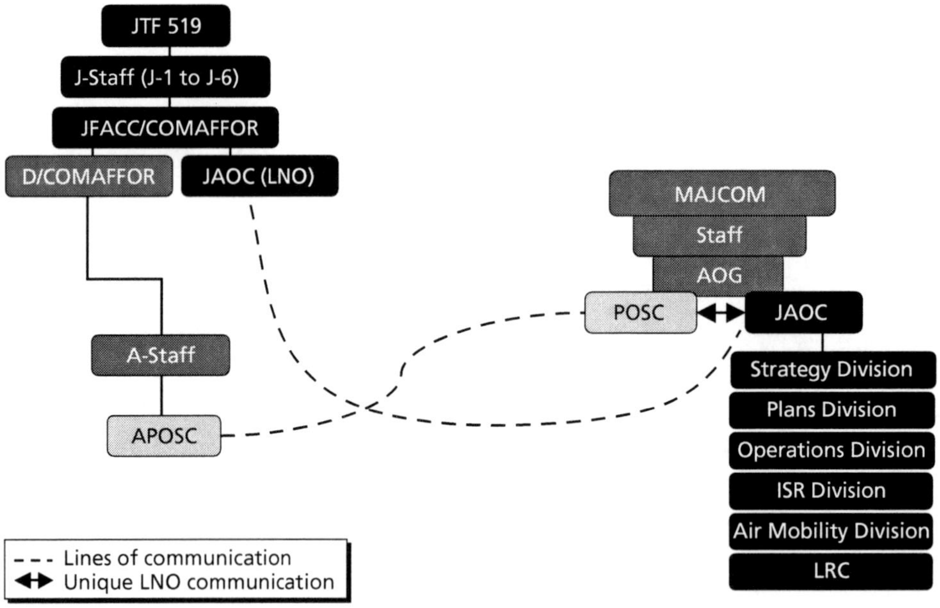

RAND TR356-A.3

AOC exercise manning provided only a small logistics element in the LRC (which the *Air and Space Commander's Handbook for the JFACC* refers to as the *logistics specialty team*). Manning constraints during TF04 minimized the number of logistics personnel in the AOC. The 502 AOG's AOC CONOPS detailed a 20-plus manned LRC led by a colonel with a lieutenant colonel deputy. However, the UTCs (7FVX1 and 7FVX5) employed during this exercise had only one logistics-specific personnel requirement. During TF04, there was only one assigned AOC logistics person (2G0X1) plus a PACAF Headquarters augmentee (2W0XX), who were then augmented by two temporary duty Air Force Reserve personnel (one each 2G and 2W) from a reserve component unit based in the U.S. mainland.

The LRC's manning level forced the logistics personnel to focus on maintaining slides and other report information (for example, cross-checking exercise data on force arrival). The LRC personnel also spent time manually entering TPFDD information and creating update and logistics status slides for the AOC.

Implications

It should be noted that the unique organizational structure used during TF04 did not break the C2 effect. Outstanding individual personnel found ways to make the organizational construct work. However, challenges did exist that could be minimized under the TO-BE architecture.

Within the operational environment of TF04, ACS activity took place across several CSC2 nodes. Tasks and responses should be coordinated across these nodes and should reference the capability that they support when possible. To accomplish this collaboration successfully in wartime, these arrangements must be clear in peacetime and practiced daily. Wartime and peacetime systems and procedures should be harmonized.

Terms should be used consistently. In TF04, component headquarters were split between forward and rear elements. Others were not split but were still referred to as being *rear*. In the future, nodes that are physically divided may be referred to as *forward* and *rear*, but nodes that are not divided, such as the PACAF POSC during TF04, should not be referred to as either. The POSC functioned as a theater-level CSC2 node with broad MAJCOM and unified combatant command component authority. It was rear only in relation to being outside the JOA. It was forward in that it represented the theater when working with the CONUS support functions. While the terms *forward* and *rear* have some meaning in this context, the way they were used during TF04 created some confusing situations because some CSC2 nodes represented some truly split organizations.

In moving to the TO-BE operational architecture, with its collaborative work processes and common shared data sets, it will become very important to understand command relationships and authority when working discrete tasks. Even though units may be split to limit forward footprints and the time it takes to build critical capability forces, split units work for a common commander within a set chain of command.

The A-4 and A-7 roles and responsibilities first became an issue during interviews with ACS personnel in several CSC2 nodes. Arriving forces need support functions from many functional elements now vested in A-4 (logistics) and A-7 (civil engineers). Joint organizations embed the civil engineering function in the J-4. Some commands within the Air Force have broken out the civil engineering function into a separate staff element, A-7, that focuses on installations.[7] If this is the case, commonly used terminology should be adopted to describe A-7 as the focal point for installations or installation support.

To fully achieve the CSC2 TO-BE operational architecture, capability reporting should transcend the functional division between A-4 and A-7. During TF04, A-7 representatives in the CPT took the lead in providing the beddown answer. The division of responsibility between A-4 and A-7 should not lead to a division in reporting base capability. A process for unifying the A-4–A-7 response could be a step toward TO-BE processes.

The advantage of 502 AOG leadership of the CPT is that it enables the planning and execution functions to merge, specifically the POSC CPC with the Strategy Division of the 56th Air and Space Operations Squadron's AOC. This is critical because no ACS personnel were assigned to the AOC Strategy Division during TF04.

The CPT represents a good process that needs strong functional support from the staff. The CPC from the POSC and the AOC Strategy Division complemented each other and worked together in a closed-loop process to produce an operationally and logistically feasible COA. Having a common file workspace to which personnel from across several nodes have access, as appropriate, would be beneficial. Having an ACS-trained person assigned to the Strategy Division could help achieve the TO-BE vision.

---

[7] AMC has moved services and civil engineering under an A-7. The command is also in the process of moving security forces under A-7.

The AOC and POSC are in close proximity, are assigned to the same parent AOG, and have a peacetime history of working together, but they were not in the same chain of command for TF04. When an Air Force commander is appointed as the JFACC (outside of Korea, which has its own AOC), the AOC is assigned operationally to the JTF/CC through the JFACC, and the POSC is assigned to and supports COMPACAF. Different organizational chains of command could lead to confusion if the TO-BE operational architecture does not make the chain of command explicitly visible across nodes.

The confusion of the lines of reporting may have been a function of the exercise. However, the physical location of the AOC on Hickam AFB may have eased AOC-to-POSC discussions at the risk of not fully involving the 13AF APOSC—COMAFFOR's peer to the AOC. However, this created the potential for parallel tasking. The leadership at PACAF was careful to keep tasking in proper channels and to offer help when asked as the theater reachback for AFFOR tasks. The structure did not preclude commanders from asking their CSC2 organizations to work their individual responses. Because of the split in responsibilities and because of the location of the AOC near the PACAF POSC, it was possible for AFFOR tasks not to receive the appropriate priority.

ACS plays a critical role in strategic thinking and planning. AOC LRC manning should better reflect the importance of the ACS role in the AOC. During TF04, AOC LRC personnel were mainly engaged in maintaining the information assurance of exercise force arrival, basing status, and inventory data. Having an experienced person embedded in the MAAP process would also facilitate applying ACS knowledge directly to the munitions challenge. The importance of the MAAP process took the few ACS personnel away from other ACS AOC tasks. This organization and level of combat support manpower put the AS-IS architecture to the test. Usually, the LRC would be able to call on deep support from the functional staff. TO-BE collaborative systems and work processes would have been one way to cope with constraints.

The assessment team also noted during TF04 that POSC's A-3 was responsible for reporting aircraft status, not A-4. Aircraft capability involves more than the availability of aircraft and crews. The maintenance status of the aircraft should have an operational and ACS context. Drilling down to the maintenance status of any one aircraft is an ACS issue. As the Air Force moves to effects-based operations and works to create capabilities for the JFC, aircraft status is actually only part of the information needed to determine the true set of capabilities the JFACC needs. In the future, ACS should work with operations and the AOC to see how best to report capabilities and enable drill-downs for specific information. Having a robust ACS presence in the deliberate planning process and during warfighting strategy meetings would help provide better support to the warfighter. The TO-BE operational architecture needs CSC2 systems that help build the analytic basis for a specific capability tied to the reality of available infrastructure, logistics, services, and the ability to sustain that capability into the future.

C2 Systems Integration and Decision-Support Tools

In the ACS area, most of the information-sharing the assessment team observed during TF04 was conducted using unclassified and secure email and telephone. Moving to the CSC2 TO-BE environment means integrating ACS information systems and products and making them available in a collaborative environment.

Observations

Our observations about the systems used to communicate knowledge between the nodes fall into the following areas:

- a common operating picture for ACS tasks
- collaborative tools
- ACS activity reporting.

A Common Operating Picture for ACS Tasks. During TF04, the assessment team observed that many tools and systems were in use. The PACOM TF04 exercise goals included evaluating some systems and tools that could be said to have TO-BE characteristics. What the team observed was an ad hoc mix of systems that differed not only across the nodes but sometimes within a CSC2 node.

Each functional area in combat support uses different systems. For example, in tracking aircraft movement, the logistics planners use the Single Mobility System (SMS), Deliberate and Crisis Planning and Execution Segments (DCAPES), Global Transportation Network, Global Air Transportation Execution System, Global Command and Control System, and Cargo Movement Operating System. Some data overlapped, but each system had a different function and provided unique data, depending on the specific situation and the initial information available.

Another issue was that different nodes used different systems to collect and format information. At the APOSC, civil engineers used Ports and Airfields, while civil engineers at the POSC used GEOReach for beddown planning. Two different nodes used two different systems with two different data sets to answer the same question. In the AOC, similar issues were apparent.

Forces identified in the operations plan had to configure their deployments quickly to take advantage of the tactical situation. Lessons learned during Serbia, Afghanistan, and Iraq indicate that AOC-directed changes occur faster than JOPES and TPFDD can be updated and validated.[8] Training was also an issue in using such tools and will be discussed in the next major section.

Collaborative Tools. One initiative to aid in data- and knowledge-sharing that PACOM tested was the use of collaborative tools, such as IWS, CAS, and Logistics Common Relevant Operational Picture (LOGCROP). LOGCROP was found to be inoperable during the training before TF04 began; therefore, it was not used during the exercise itself. Afloat personnel successfully used CAS as a C2 tool for monitoring, assessing, and planning. Specifically, CAS was used to post task lists, briefings, and an event log. CAS was not used in the other nodes.

The JTF staff afloat and 13AF used IWS; however, exercise constraints may have limited the application of IWS.

---

[8] See Tripp et al. (2002) and Lynch et al. (2005).

ACS Activity Reporting. In addition to the use of different systems at different nodes, reporting from the nodes also differed. Assessment team members were told that the criteria for reporting ACS functional elements and capability status were different during the TF04 exercise from peacetime operation, which may also be different from those for an actual contingency. For example, the APOSC may report civil engineering as fully operational at a base, while the POSC may report only initial operational capability.

During TF04, the POSC operated as a supporting organization, staying informed about exercise operations but was not directly involved in the day-to-day missions in the JOA. Twice a day, update briefings were given in the POSC. In observing the daily briefs, the assessment team noted the method of reporting logistics information. Instead of reporting the capabilities that were available or necessary to support a mission, the status of the support was reported. For instance, the number of aircraft that were not mission capable was reported, not the level of capability of the remaining aircraft. Reporting was similar for fuels and munitions. This required the commander to provide the operational context himself or to ask follow-on questions. Rolling up functional reporting and connecting individual inputs to the capabilities the data support will greatly simplify this process for commanders. It will also help gauge changes in status with the change in the status of the capability it supports. Several times, functional representatives were asked what the effect on the projected ATO would be. ACS personnel need systems and tools in the TO-BE that will readily help them gauge the consequences of these changes.

Another example was the beddown planning that was considered for alternative locations. Instead of being told how many people could be fed at each base, base capacity could have been reported. In the reports given during the exercise, excess capacity was not readily apparent to the decisionmaker. The decisionmaker had to determine how the information affected overall capability.

Implications

In moving to the TO-BE architecture, peacetime procedures should be integrated with wartime processes and systems to create a common operating picture for all nodes. During TF04, while the APOSC and the POSC simultaneously worked two individual beddown assessments, having two different systems for conducting beddown assessment could be problematic. If the task had flowed from the APOSC to support from the POSC, the systems might not have been able to communicate information, causing duplication of effort. This could be explained by the high cost of populating databases, which drives the use of existing databases maintained at centralized locations, such as Ports and Airfields. Ready access to centralized databases results in frequent use.

Tools should be developed for accessing data elements from different integration systems. Having so many systems makes gathering data time-consuming. Then, the resulting data should be presented in a user-friendly format that would include the ability to create PowerPoint slides. Machine-to-machine reporting could allow ACS personnel to monitor and detect patterns of use so that shortages could be addressed in real time. Having a common relational database for ACS would help build and maintain a common operating picture to improve combat support activities.

Collaborative tools could have enhanced the AS-IS operational architecture C2 and should be employed in the future. For a tool like IWS to be used effectively, it needs a vision and a history of regular use in peacetime to reinforce the shared nature of the work processes and should permit adjustment of the processes according to the workload and manning at each node. Without proper training, personnel can become lost in the maze of virtual rooms and organizations. Incorporating a tool like IWS into initial and follow-on technical training, as appropriate, would be beneficial.

Collaborative work processes are not fully understood in the AS-IS workplace. For example, creating a common server storage area for storage of key work files and final products was being used, but not to the extent that it overcame the limitations of the AS-IS system and work processes.[9] The TO-BE architecture needs a deliberate, well-thought-out IM plan. This plan needs to be visible across all the CSC2 nodes. Documents and data need to be clearly labeled, with access to an archive for superseded information.

Reporting should be standardized across CSC2 nodes. Currently, when readiness slides are briefed in the AS-IS operational architecture, there is no accepted, objective measure of what the different levels of readiness represent. The current reporting structure relies on subjective analysis or criteria, which, if not defined by the parent or user organization, is left to the unit commander. Too often, these criteria are stripped from the data that are presented to a decisionmaker and thus lack the full context of the report. The TO-BE vision should try to make the criteria more visible and should report within a capability context the decisionmaker readily understands.

For a linear work process, such as today's AS-IS operational architecture, this may work, but the TO-BE requires a more-common reporting capability. At the least, TO-BE user-defined formats need the capability to drill down into the data—dynamically—to present a full understanding of what the formatted data is depicting. Commanders need to grasp information quickly and build knowledge about the ACS and the operational situation. It may not be realistic to expect the format to be 100-percent common because knowledge-gathering is a personal experience and because CSC2 nodes ultimately work for their own commanders. However, some standardization is not only prudent but necessary if the required CSC2 performance across nodes is to be realized. Common formats in the TO-BE will ensure that commanders are viewing the same depiction and can discuss it without confusion in a crisis situation.

Informed decisions about missions and forces require complete comparisons of the available quantities of commodities against the requirements. Receiving only the numbers of aircraft and the amounts of fuel available requires the decisionmaker to perform his or her own capability analysis. Instead of the number of mission-capable aircraft, it would be more useful to know how the maintenance issues would affect the ability to complete the mission. For example, would a flying mission have to be cancelled? Since the POSC was a reachback element in this exercise, it could have performed the capability analyses and provided the results to the logistics personnel in the APOSC and/or the AOC. Excess capabilities can be just as or

---

[9] For TF04, JTF 519 maintained a common work area in which files were stored for general reference by staff and components.

more important than limiting factors. The important issue is the overall effect of information on the mission objectives and the commander's intent.

Training and Education

The exercise design itself may have affected the use of collaborative tools and systems.

Observations
Our observations on training and education fall into the following areas:

- collaborative tools and systems
- exercise design.

Collaborative Tools and Systems. Some nodes used newsgroups and chat rooms, two more first-generation TO-BE capabilities, but not all personnel were aware of these capabilities. Few of these systems were used with deliberate purpose as part of the core work process, which was to be expected given that TF04 illustrated the use of the AS-IS operational architecture. Only one of the AOC LRC–assigned personnel was familiar with the newsgroup capability and its use in a collaborative workspace. Access to and understanding of an IWS-like capability would be beneficial.

For classified telecommunications, most workstations in the POSC have legacy red-switch telephones. Other nodes had STU III telephones. According to some POSC personnel, communications between the red-switch telephone and STU III are complicated. Other personnel claimed that the red-switch telephones were easy to use. To realize better integration with operations as called for in the TO-BE operational architecture, personnel working ACS tasks will need better access to or better understanding of secure means of communication.

Exercise Design. Current exercise designs do not fully support the expeditionary combat support training objectives because of the inability to simulate strategic air and surface deployment, logistics in-transit visibility, sustainment requirements, and the replication of organizations not participating in the training audience. During TF04, PACOM joint and Air Force logistics personnel were part of the exercise planning effort and were included in planning conferences and designing the scenario. However, many ACS activities are simulated, and exercise scenarios generally focus on the execution phase of military exercises, which does not fully stress ACS planning and deployment. A modeling and simulation capability to project future requirements would be beneficial in enabling proactive, rather than reactive, ACS.[10]

The TF04 design provided many challenges for the training audience to overcome. Several newsgroup messages posted on the exercise Web site highlighted the player audience's frustration in trying to determine whether a given unit had arrived in theater and was ready

---

[10] Many of the core PACAF logistics personnel were dual-hatted as members of the PACOM standing JTF and were deployed either as the JTF staff or component staff afloat. This took the core PACAF logistics experience away from the POSC and PACAF staff.

to operate. Adjudication was handled by having the response cell acknowledge the arrival and readiness of units for combat in the appropriate newsgroups.

OSCs rely on a variety of systems (DCAPES, SMS, the Global Decision Support System, the Global Transportation Network, etc.) to track scheduling and movement of units. Monitoring these systems from validation through reception and staging, then onward movement and integration (when required), is part of the complete picture the OSC should be prepared to provide the AFFOR and MAJCOM commander. Other strategic deployment processes not exercised during TF04 included sourcing, level IV detail on air and sea schedules, and the inability to dynamically change the flow of forces into the JOA because of changes in the environment. During the validation process of TF04, it was assumed all Air Force units in the deliberately planned TPFDD were available at the time of execution. In the real world, however, a rapid runway repair team had to be sourced through the AEF Center because the team had been deployed out of theater. The POSC worked through A-1 and through the AEF Center to task (simulated) replacements. However, these changes were neither reflected in the plan identification designator nor visible to the newsgroups.

Implications

The opportunity to observe TF04 helped to build knowledge about ACS processes and the need for CSC2 systems that enable the TO-BE architecture. The operational environment of TF04 stressed ACS activities in ways that crossed functional boundaries. TF04 also called for deep knowledge of how ACS functions and skills contribute to the capabilities that are being provided to the JFC/CC. This was an excellent operational environment in which to observe an AS-IS system responding to some characteristics that will also exist in the TO-BE. In moving to the TO-BE architecture, ACS transformation strategies need to create opportunities for personnel to better understand the role of ACS in creating warfighting capabilities and should make a deliberate and affirming effort to train current and future personnel in TO-BE tools, equipment, and analytic processes. This needs the shaping influence of a robust local training program in each node and a firm foundation of formal training in TO-BE systems.

Current expeditionary operations demand proactive personnel who are able to anticipate JFC, JFACC, and AFFOR needs. Ensuring that personnel have the necessary skills, experience, and knowledge to achieve the TO-BE architecture requires a robust and adaptive process for training and education. Training and education start with a strong ACS foundation laid down in formal Air Force courses that is then augmented with deliberate and well-thought-out means of practicing and learning while performing everyday ACS tasks. Observing the AS-IS state, under TF04-generated operational stresses, provided a window into just how important quality training experiences are for the TO-BE operational architecture.

Participating fully, understanding the planning assumptions and their effects on the ACS infrastructure available to support a plan, and seeing ACS equipment and personnel not in terms of inventory and location but for their potential to create a warfighting capability is necessary. This will take training, practice, and regular dialogue with operations.

In moving from the AS-IS to the TO-BE architecture, it is imperative that CSC2 personnel in all specialties receive the necessary background education in AOC operations, JTF deliberate planning, and the potential for the TO-BE operational architecture to shape the combat capability the COMAFFOR provides. NCOs and officers under the TO-BE architecture will be called on to fuse functional data and information and apply their knowledge to the COMAFFOR/JFACC problems. This commitment to education will provide more fully qualified NCOs or officers who are confident of their contribution and who know how best to apply ACS qualities in creating capabilities.

The assessment team noted that much of the success of the TF04 exercise hinged on the placement of combat forces prior to operations. This crucial phase of deployment and employment was not practiced or included in exercise play. If ACS personnel are not trained to support deliberate planning processes and are not given the opportunity to test their knowledge and skills in a realistic way in all phases of operations, they will first be put to the test during an actual crisis. CSC2 systems and analytic decision support tools are needed at all levels for the value of the TO-BE architecture to be fully realized.

All nodes should have the ability to train during peacetime as they would operate in war, using the same systems. These systems (or replications of them) should be employed during exercises to maximize training opportunities. Peacetime activity needs to be modeled and displayed so that TO-BE personnel will recognize patterns as they develop and be in a mental position that drives the resolution of problems without constraining the desired warfighting capability. Just knowing the contribution of discrete ACS tasks and activities that support the warfighter could have major ramifications as ACS professional NCOs and officers apply their expertise more precisely.

Summary of Recommendations

Today, the Air Force finds itself deployed around the globe, often on short notice and with resources stretched to the breaking point. Movement toward the CSC2 TO-BE operational architecture will help improve C2 through better systems, tools, machine-to-machine data exchanges, and a standardized organizational structure that all ACS personnel are familiar with. This improvement in C2 will enhance the ability to provide ACS to the COMAFFOR in support of the joint warfighter.

The assessment team used TF04 to generate combat support issues that crossed CSC2 nodes. The PACOM exercise deployed joint, joint component, and Air Force senior leadership with tailored C2, providing the operational environment from which the assessment team identified a range of issues affected by the TO-BE operational architecture. These issues included organization, leadership, personnel, doctrine, and training.

Following is a summary of the specific recommendations of the assessment team in response to its observations and knowledge of the TO-BE operational architecture.

Organizational Structure
Clearly define command relationships, including roles and responsibilities

- between nodes (APOSC/POSC and APOSC/AOC)
- within nodes (A-staffs)

- within virtual collaborative workspaces.

Integrate combat support planning with the operational campaign planning process by

- improving integration of AFFOR capabilities and processes into the AOC
- integrating combat support personnel into all AOC divisions, specifically, the Strategy and Plans Divisions.

C2 Systems Integration and Decision-Support Tools

Establish a common system architecture for all nodes by

- incorporating efficient and effective tools including collaborative tools that accommodate joint and commercial systems requirements
- adapting and use for peacetime management
- promoting ACS professional analysis capability at each level.

Standardize data reporting criteria across nodes (data quality, assurance, and format) by

- enabling users to extract common shared data onto forms and formats that help tee up information for decisionmakers
- allowing dynamic reporting with drill-down capability so users can drill down into data to build trust and confidence in the data picture and to allow the key factors constraining warfighting capabilities to become visible to ACS professionals.

Training and Education

Initiate CSC2 training into existing courses or as a stand-alone course, as required. Peacetime training should mirror contingency demands and wartime operations.

APPENDIX B
Austere Challenge 2004 Case Study

As the Air Force began to transition to the TO-BE operational architecture, AF/ILG was tasked to assess the path to implementation. Austere Challenge 2004 (AC04), a USAFE exercise held January through March 2004, provided an opportunity to observe the TO-BE architecture at important CSC2 nodes in an operational environment. The Chairman of the Joint Chiefs of Staff sponsored AC04. The exercise was directed and scheduled by EUCOM and conducted by USAFE as a warfighter training event. The exercise scenario and supporting simulated environment were developed and run by the WPC facility at Einsedlerhof Air Station, near Ramstein AB, which is maintained jointly by USAFE and the U.S. Army Europe Command. An annual C2 exercise, Austere Challenge was designed to exercise a USAFE operational plan or a COA. The USAFE Commander also used AC04 to validate a notional warfighting headquarters structure operating within a JTF. The JTF air component structure was supported by a theaterwide COMAFFOR staff.

The assessment team used the AC04 operational environment to observe the CSC2 nodes and information flows in relation to the TO-BE operational architecture and to explore the integration of combat support systems and processes. AC04 provided an operational environment for comparing the AS-IS CSC2 operational architecture with the proposed TO-BE architecture under stress. Using exercise topics as a focus, the assessment team reviewed how information flowed between and within nodes, what systems were used, and how personnel involved in the topic of focus were trained. This report is not an assessment of AC04. The exercise simply offered an opportunity to observe ACS tasks within an operational context of a major C2 exercise. The CSC2 assessment team did not attempt to change or interfere with the exercise scenario or USAFE exercise goals. The exercise provided a unique opportunity to observe a range of CSC2 nodes involved in executing the scenario, such as COMAFFOR/ JFACC, an AFFOR staff (the engaged NAF, 16AF), the AOC, and the MAJCOM theater-wide organization (AFEUR). The exercise scenario involved forces from both CAF and MAF providers, with MAF and sustainment elements embedded in the AOC and AFFOR staff organizations.

The assessment of movement toward the TO-BE CSC2 operational architecture during AC04 was successful. The AC04 exercise schedule was accelerated by a month and divided into three phases. In addition, the training audience's organizational structure did not exist prior to the exercise. Personnel had to be identified, trained, and quickly organized into the exercise warfighting structure. With these changes, there were challenges in the exercise simulation that did not fully fit the exercise goals. The ability of the training audience to quickly adapt to these changes and gain the knowledge necessary for the exercise to be a success was remarkable.

AC04 was a USAFE command post exercise, not a field exercise. Organizations above or outside the USAFE MAJCOM and 16AF did not participate.[1] The WPC simulated forces below the operational level. The training audience consisted of the JFACC and staff, the AFFOR staff, the AOC, and the AFEUR.[2] Because of this level of participation, force-level inputs were simulated, certain functions were not performed, and/or scripted responses were given to queries. The artificiality of the exercise also created other issues, such as reporting inconsistencies. When the exercise environment itself was responsible for a problem or concern, it is noted in the report.

AC04, as a EUCOM-directed and USAFE-conducted exercise, was limited to the scenario as scripted. The scenario created some organizational challenges that may not apply in other theaters. In addition to the exercise goals, the USAFE commander asked USAFE/IG to help validate the AFEUR organization and tasks. When appropriate, this assessment used these tasks to help define the scope and purpose of the exercise training audience.

Organizational Structure

The AF/IL CSC2 TO-BE architecture provides an organizational construct for ensuring that C2 functions are performed through a standard or uniform arrangement of personnel, equipment, communications, facilities, and procedures throughout the Air Force. Figure B.1 illustrates the current understanding of suggested nodes in the TO-BE CSC2 operational architecture. The CSC2 construct that the COMAFFOR employs enables planning, directing, coordinating, and controlling forces and combat support operations in its role as a service component to the JFC. It is recognized, though not obvious in the figure below, that both the AOC and the A-staff perform ACS tasks.[3]

Observations

The objectives of the assessment team were to observe how the CSC2 TO-BE organizational construct should be employed and to assess its effectiveness. Because the AC04 exercise design

---

[1] There were participants from the other EUCOM service commands and NATO. Their participation was limited to the context of the training audience. The WPC or Air Force role players simulated the participation of other JTFs, EUCOM, national leadership, and the other JTF components.

[2] The AFEUR is a new organizational construct tied to the future warfighting headquarters initiative. Its core originated in the former UTASC augmented by functional areas from the USAFE staff. The AFEUR was designed to be the theater-wide provider of forces for this exercise, commanded by a general officer reporting to the USAFE Commander.

[3] Several documents outline various levels of ACS work in the AOC. The Falconer AOC's *Flight Manual* details a logistics team that works with the Strategy Division and the MAAP Cell within the Plans Division. The Air Force *Air and Space Commander's Handbook for the JFACC* (U.S. Air Force, 2003a) outlines the AOC task flow process and inputs and outputs that integrate logistics and combat support capability to define the combat power available for employment. USAFE documents also outline a logistics presence in the AOC.

Figure B.1
TO-BE CSC2 Organizational Structure

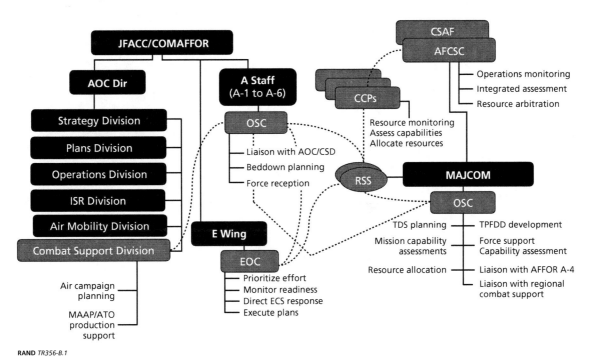

RAND TR356-B.1

focused on theater operations employment and certification of the notional USAFE warfighting organization, the assessment team was not able to assess all organizations performing ACS tasks. Several CSC2 nodes were outside the training audience and were simulated, with the node input coming from an exercise role player.[4] The assessment team's primary focus was on how the COMAFFOR/JFACC operational AFFOR (16AF) interacted with the AOC and with the HQ USAFE theaterwide AFFOR (AFEUR). Activities associated with Air Force CCPs and the Air Force CSC nodes did not receive any exercise play during AC04.

Our observations fall into the following areas:

- warfighting headquarters construct
- A-staff responsibilities
- force beddown and sustainment
- AOC location and manpower considerations.

Warfighting Headquarters Construct. The organizational construct in place during AC04 was transitional. USAFE is recasting itself as a warfighting headquarters, a transformational concept the Air Force is adopting in which headquarters and staffs can change from peacetime operations to wartime operations almost immediately. As USAFE makes this transition, the

---

[4] Assessment team members sought to overcome this limitation by initiating dialog with the WPC role-player community that supported the exercise.

AFEUR, a new organization, has been established as the C2 node for air and space operations in Europe. Figure B.2 illustrates the current transitional organizational construct.

During this exercise, the main C2 elements employed were all on Ramstein AB or in the surrounding military community. The WPC built and maintained the exercise environment. The COMAFFOR/JFACC, the deputy COMAFFOR, the AOC director, the operational AFFOR (16AF), and the theater AFFOR (AFEUR) were all in different locations, but all on Ramstein. The AOC and the operational AFFOR were collocated in the same complex on Ramstein. The exercise JOA was predominately in the 16AF AOR. The 16AF/CC acted as the COMAFFOR, and the 16AF staff acted as the operational AFFOR staff. Figure B.3 illustrates the C2 structure used during AC04.

While some organizational chains of command were still evolving during Phase II of AC04 (February), reporting structures were well established and specifically detailed by Phase III (March). The *Sixteenth Air Force Deployed Combat Staffs Concept of Operations* (16AF, 2003)

Figure B.2
USAFE March 2004 Interim Organizational Construct

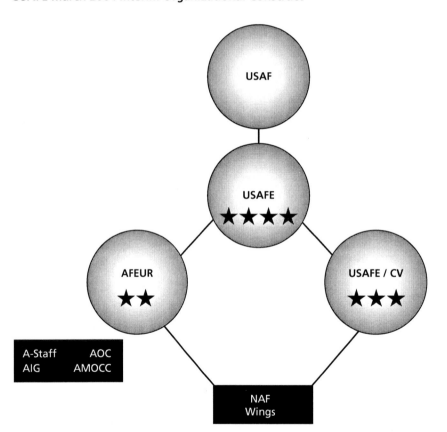

SOURCE: Isherwood (2004), slide 11.
RAND *TR356-B.2*

Figure B.3
Austere Challenge 2004 Organizational Structure

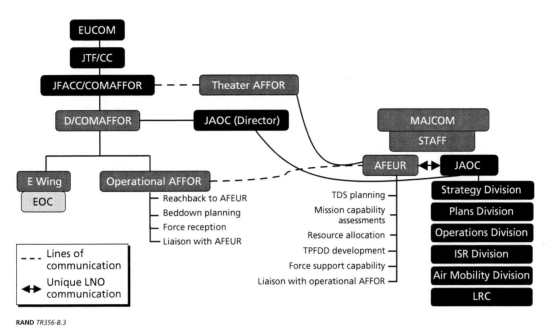

RAND *TR356-B.3*

detailed C2 from the operational (or forward) AFFOR perspective.[5] The AFFOR Command and Control CONOPS discussed C2 from the COMAFFOR and the AOC perspective. The AOC's in-flight guide (USAFE, 2004) also gave specific direction for reporting responsibilities within the AOC. CONOPs for the AFEUR have not been developed, but staff had a clear understanding of their reporting chain of command.[6]

A-Staff Responsibilities. Within the AFEUR, there was clear definition of the role and responsibilities of the A-staff.[7] The AFEUR has an A-staff configured in accordance with Air Force Doctrine Document 2. However, the civil engineering and services functions have moved from A-4 (Logistics) to create a separate A-7 (Civil Engineering) staff. This move was driven by lessons learned from Operations Enduring Freedom and Iraqi Freedom, which highlighted the need to focus on installations and basing. Discussions are under way about increasing the scope of the A-7 directorate to include all functions that fall under the Mission Support Group at the wing level. In addition, an A-9 directorate was created to provide a continuous improvement, documentation collection, and historical archive section for the AFEUR staff. The A-8 function is not defined.

---

[5] 16AF served as the air component staff to a EUCOM-formed JTF. The JTF was role played by exercise control personnel or simulation.

[6] The guide was developed and published by the USAFE 32 AOG IM staff.

[7] An "A-staff" is organized along the lines of the Joint Staff's "J-staff." USAFE used the term to divide responsibility for warfighting tasks from what were referred to as U.S. Code Title 10 tasks. For AC04, the A-staff primarily came from what was then called the USAFE Theater Aerospace Support Center (UTASC) (a CAT-like staff function), and functional representation came from the USAFE headquarters staff.

AFEUR A-4 personnel man an LRC. A-7 personnel staff the installation readiness cell (IRC). Both the LRC and IRC are within the AFEUR, which operates 24 hours a day, seven days a week with representation from all A-staffs. Generally, information and taskings flow from AFEUR's LRC or IRC to the A-4 or A-7 staffs. The LRC and IRC work closely because many of their taskings have overlapping responsibilities. These may need to be clarified before moving into a TO-BE architecture, in which work should be more collaborative and may be accomplished at more than one node.

Within the 16AF staff, roles and responsibilities were similarly well defined, and its exercise role was similar to its current approach to work. Beginning with Phase II (February), the 16AF staff imitated the AFEUR staff in separating the A-4 and A-7 functions, splitting off services and the civil engineers. For 16AF, the change was not permanent but only for the exercise.

Because the role of 16AF was well defined, it could assist AOC logistics personnel when exercise data and exercise play became intense during Phase III. It helped that both the AOC and the operational AFFOR were in the same compound. For the TO-BE architecture to be effective, this strong relationship may have to evolve within an electronic workspace with no face-to-face contact. A few days into Phase III, the AOC IM team changed the information workspace in a way that helped build a closer working relationship between the AOC and forward staff functions. TO-BE characteristics need to include cross-nodal communications structures to realize the desired behaviors.

Force Beddown and Sustainment. The AFEUR staff includes an expeditionary site planning cell. During peacetime, this cell identifies, researches, and assesses potential beddown locations. It also maintains site surveys and a database of potential beddown locations. During wartime, this cell acts as the core from which the logistics planning team (LPT) is built. The LPT is not a standing organization, but a team of functional area experts that come together when a combat support issue needs to be addressed. Although it lacks a published CONOPS, the LPT is well organized and structured. The AS-IS beddown planning process is moving toward a TO-BE vision through the introduction of automated tools (such as an Expeditionary Site Planning Portal [ESP2], which will be discussed in the next major section) and improved communications capabilities with teams sent to survey potential beddown sites.

During AC04 Phase III, a logistics officer was positioned in the AOC Strategy Division to help refine the force beddown strategy and incorporate it into AOC products and services. It is important to note that, while each node needs to be able to observe data, work, and communicate with each other, the work at each node has differing demands. Fieldwork at a potential base focuses on capturing data and assessing potential use. Work in the AOC Strategy Division concentrates on the consequences of various beddown locations for shaping the combat force and the selection of the one that enables the commander's strategy. Work in the AFFOR is more stafflike, aimed at creating Air Force capabilities and solving sustainment issues to maintain the capabilities over time. In moving to the TO-BE architecture, each node not only needs to have common means for sharing and working together with the other nodes but also needs discrete decision tools that are aimed at its specific work tasks.

Within the A-4 and A-7 staff at the operational AFFOR (16AF), a base expert was identified for each assigned base to be the central point of contact for any issues involving that base during the exercise. This created a node for accumulating knowledge about a base. Base experts could talk to other base experts and quickly resolve combat support issues that appeared as the exercise progressed. They became facilitators who could build cross-functional solutions to specific problems caused by the exercise play.

AOC Location and Manning Considerations. Collocated nodes could pass information directly to one another, skipping other important nodes in the C2 chain of command. During AC04, physical proximity of the AOC and AFEUR did not seem to lead to this problem. Most often, the requests for information flowed from the AOC to the operational AFFOR, who would then reach back to the theater AFFOR when necessary. The assessment team did find one instance in which AOC personnel reached directly back to the AFEUR, but this was an anomaly, not the norm. This was most likely because of their familiarity with the AFEUR personnel, having worked with them before. In the TO-BE architecture, tasks may be performed by personnel in several nodes, emphasizing the importance of well-defined responsibilities and authority.

The fact that the operational AFFOR staff was organized and had a history of working together helped inspire AOC trust and confidence in the information. Close proximity gave the JFACC/COMAFFOR access to functional combat support experts. There was a period during Phase III when the munitions data being used for ATO production was being questioned (a MAAP Tool Kit, TBMCS, and data simulation problem). Working closely with the AOC Combat Plans Division logistics personnel, the operational AFFOR's A-4 was able to help them gain confidence in the data set and work a joint solution to better report and feed TBMCS with the correct data. Having ready, on-site access to the component, A-4 and A-7 helped the AOC find a workaround solution in combat plans.

Logistics personnel were scarce in the AOC. Most combat support personnel were manipulating data, verifying data, or creating PowerPoint slides. The 32 AOG, in organizing and running the USAFE AOC, did recognize the value of having logistics personnel in the Strategy Division. The Falconer AOC's *Flight Manual* also recognizes this importance when it discusses the logistics team and their organization to help shape the combat capability.

Implications

The roles, missions, duties, and responsibilities of each C2 node—the operational and theater AFFORs and the AOC—were fairly well defined in this new AFEUR construct.

Although fairly well defined, the roles and missions of each staff element and node should be clearly defined to prevent confusion and duplication of effort and to ensure efficient use of resources. This will be more crucial in the TO-BE work environment, in which reachback could become reach forward or when tasks performed off site are not firmly anchored to an office of primary responsibility. Our observations found that collocation, allowing face-to-face interaction, is valued when the situation is less defined or when communications nodes are less robust.

It was interesting to observe the effect of location and position within the JTF and/or COMAFFOR structure during AC04. When under AC04 operational stress, the nodes in the training audience worked well across nodes as their roles and responsibilities became more definite. When a problem arose early in the exercise, the node with more information visibility generally stepped in to deal with the issue. As the nodes became more confident and as systems better supported the information requirements at each site, operations evened out.

Depending on where an ACS person sits, CSC2 demands are different. Work demands and the information different nodes need can be different for personnel in the field, in the AOC, in a staff CAT or LPT, or working from a staff position in the AFFOR. TO-BE systems need to enable common access to shared data and to the value-added information generated at each node, but they also must enable personnel working discrete tasks endemic to each CSC2 node.

C2 Systems Integration and Decision-Support Tools

In the ACS arena, most of the information-sharing the assessment team observed during AC04 took place via unclassified and secure email and telephone. Moving to the CSC2 TO-BE environment means integrating ACS information systems and products and having them available to all ACS stakeholders in a collaborative environment.

Observations

Our observations about the systems used to communicate knowledge between the nodes fall into the following areas:

- a common operating picture
- collaborative tools and strategies and ACS work processes.

A Common Operating Picture. A common operating picture integrates information from several sources into a single picture in real or near-real time. This enables decisionmakers access to information to aid in making informed decisions.

The TO-BE architecture calls for the ability of personnel at each node to assess and query data sets to build knowledge within ACS. The AS-IS common operating picture for the ACS system, as observed during AC04, was a simple PowerPoint presentation that provided a daily logistics snapshot for the warfighter. These daily presentations were archived on the organization's server for later reference for trend analysis.

Work processes also affect the building of a common operating picture for ACS systems. How people gain the necessary data and add value during the internode collaboration process is key to fully realizing the power of a common picture. During AC04, even when information was available across nodes for work, it was necessary for personnel to call or email to gain the necessary assurances that the information was current. This need for feedback was eased somewhat by the creation of an IM plan, first across the AOC and operational AFFOR staff and later between these two forward units and the theater-level AFFOR. This relatively simple step provided personnel with a stable organizational structure in which they could quickly distinguish between current and draft information products, as well as a reliable place to find the necessary information. This step effectively created an electronic workspace with sufficient structure and information visibility that work productivity within the AC04 training audience improved significantly.

Collaborative Tools and Strategies and ACS Work Processes. The AS-IS Falconer AOC has fairly advanced collaborative tools aimed at accessing and working with common data sets available to personnel in the AOC; the AFFOR staff has fewer tools. However, even in the AOC, very few of these tools have been applied to ACS tasks. A mission application like the MAAP Tool Kit bundles together program applications that automatically build worksheets and transfer information into other applications. Any ACS-tasked personnel who needed to sort through large data sets, such as personnel, fuels, or munitions tracking data, could use that basic capability.

Likewise, specific functions have grown in the AOC to help manage and qualify intelligence among the various intelligence, surveillance, and reconnaissance (ISR) nodes for the COMAFFOR/JFACC. Processing, exploitation, and dissemination (PED) are accomplished by a combination of distributed work task assignments and reachback to specific intelligence products and services. A dedicated team in the ISR Division, working across federated intelligence organizations, maintains the integrity of the collaborative ISR work. Its work is supported by tools that allow it to maintain JFACC visibility over tasking of nodes with AOC-needed information.

Almost all communications between the operational and theater AFFORs and the AOC are point-to-point, using secure (for example, the STU III telephone, STE, or SIPRNET) or nonsecure (for example, unclassified telephones or NIPRNET email) lines of communication—all one-to-one. Personnel were using unit or user-defined Excel spreadsheets and PowerPoint slides. This improved rapidly once the IM community developed a TO-BE–like deliberate process for IM, the AOC's in-flight guide (USAFE, 2004).[8] The second major factor affecting collaborative workspace was the strong division and command enforcement of the IM plan during AC04 Phase III.

By the end of AC04, Web sites were being used more effectively to integrate and direct AOC and operational AFFOR personnel to current data and work files. Web sites were not used to support the theater or operational AFFOR or the AOC. Only the AFEUR A-3 personnel who used JOPES had a newsgroup for data sharing. The operational AFFOR staff did not have direct access to any combat support information systems, such as CAMS, CAS, or the Fuels Automated System, greatly limiting their ability to build or access a common collaborative data system for unit-level data. The operational AFFOR Staff was not familiar with the combat support information available on NIPRNET through Global Combat Support System–Air Force (GCSS-AF) or the Air Force Portal. The theater AFFOR staff did have access to some combat support information systems and appeared to be more familiar with

---

[8] Once the AOC IM staff completed the task of building and maintaining an IM structure in the AOC and operational AFFOR, the proximity of the AFEUR servers also allowed the staff to do the same for the AFEUR. As AC04 concluded, the AOC IM staff was also applying the knowledge it gained from working with these three organizations to WPC exercise control IM. Role-player information became much better organized and more consistently Web linked. This immediately smoothed JFC-to-JFACC and theater AFFOR-to-AFEUR (EUCOM) and force unit–to–operational AFFOR exercise play. It became more apparent which were actual exercise challenges and which were problems created by the simulation and/or exercise control work process.

the kinds of combat support information available on NIPRNET through GCSS-AF or the Air Force Portal. No knowledge-management function appeared to be in use at the theater or operational AFFOR or the AOC until relatively late in the exercise. Not having access to a PED-like management tool limited the ability of commanders, functional managers, and directors to gain sufficient trust and confidence in collaborative and distributed tasking during AC04.

The AOC eventually did have a detailed knowledge-management function with clear guidelines, a Web site for posting information, and specific reporting requirements. The sophistication of the IM application approached a TO-BE level of service. By the end of the exercise, this success began to affect performance across the training audience and in exercise control–provided functions.

USAFE A-4 has taken the lead in the development of an ESP2. The vision for the ESP2 is to provide war planners a one-stop collaborative decision-support system to facilitate timely and thorough analysis and assessments of sites based on preexisting site surveys, airfield databases, and authoritative information sources. The 32 AOG IM also set up an AC04 portal and electronic work structure that was very helpful in managing the flow of AOC products.

Additionally, portions of the AFEUR A-staff functions were setting up newsgroups for information-sharing. The AOC Time Critical Targeting cell was using some chat capabilities and other TO-BE–like collaboration capabilities. However, IWS would be a valuable resource for the AFFOR staff to facilitate cross-functional communications and coordination to provide insight on the health of the organizations.

Implications

The designation of an authoritative source for key C2 information, for example, fuel supply and munitions expended, did not appear to have been determined prior to the exercise. An in-flight guide was provided during the exercise to supply some collaborative structure between AOC divisions and was later supplemented with an online structure for use within the operational context of AC04.

In fact, the assessment team's observations during AC04 suggest that a common operating picture is a key enabling capability for moving to the TO-BE operational architecture. Without a PED-like ACS capability (discussed above), it would be difficult for a forward commander to gain trust and confidence in a system that relied on ACS tasks being accomplished by organizations not under his or her direct control or even using expertise in a reachback mode. A common operating picture will also help error detection and problem solving to add value either in terms of precision or timeliness. The fact that this is routinely done within the intelligence community using PED and a deliberate IM structure implies that this CSC2 TO-BE quality would be obtainable in the near future for ACS-tasked organizations.

The AC04 AOC had clear guidelines for file storage and naming conventions for reports. The AFEUR had a standardized briefing slide format that fulfilled the AS-IS expectations for a common operating picture for ACS systems. However, the data requirements and format for the daily JFC and COMAFFOR/JFACC briefings did not appear to have been determined before the exercise started.[9] Refinement of the staff processes at each echelon of command would be beneficial. Information collection and integration schemes should be defined for all areas. Within the vertical AFFOR staff functions, defining an office of primary responsibility for each information requirement would be helpful. AC04 shows that making this office visible across Air Force ACS, along with key information about the task, is essential in building the necessary ACS collaborative and distributed work community. The office of primary responsibility should have a plan or procedure for sharing that information with its vertically aligned counterparts, as well as with other AFFOR staff functions that may use that information. Likewise, because the Falconer AOC logistics team acknowledged that collaboration with the AFFOR staff is its primary source of logistics information, the logistics team needs to have the same access to ACS-focused program tools, services, and infrastructure that is provided others in the AOC. This capability should reach beyond the AOC and AFFOR staff to theater-level organizations, ACS distributed work centers (when they begin to exist), and Air Force reachback organizations in CONUS. Horizontal information-sharing should take place at each echelon of command with a common operating picture for ACS systems. The authoritative source for information should be defined within the vertical AFFOR-staff (theater and JTF component) functions and should be defined for each echelon of command.

AC04 observations made it clear that the ACS community has great power when working together. Having a deliberate process for sharing the information each node creates is part of realizing this potential.

Training and Education

The AFEUR was recently certified as USAFE's warfighting headquarters and is fast becoming a leader in establishing a formal training program for assigned personnel, as well as those in battle staff augmentation positions. Perhaps because AC04's construct was new at the start of the exercise, much of the focus during AC04 was on training and education, especially for the two AFFOR staffs. The COMAFFOR is the lead for outlining how Air Force units and organizations meet the JFC's warfighting requirements. This includes how CSC2 connects and supports the ongoing joint warfighting operations and support structure. The Air Force, as an institution, is responsible for providing the combat capability foundation that the COMAFFOR provides the specific JFC. Unfortunately, the training audience did not include supporting ACS capabilities outside USAFE. In the TO-BE architecture, it will be important to build experience and to train as an enterprise.

The assessment team participated in some of the early planning conferences devoted to creating the new organization and building a sufficiently robust exercise environment to adequately test the new structure. The training audience during AC04 was the theater COMAFFOR, theater COMAFFOR staff, JTF component AOC, and JTF COMAFFOR

---

[9] This may be because the AFEUR did not exist prior to the exercise. As mentioned elsewhere in this report, the AFEUR was a new organization during AC04, and its core manpower was drawn from the UTASC and functional MAJCOM staff.

staff. The assessment team observed some of the earliest training and attended training sessions during each exercise phase. The initial AFFOR and AOC integration training sessions were conducted during and just after these initial planning meetings. Many of these briefings became the baseline documentation for the AFEUR and AOC operations.

AC04 created a new organization, the AFEUR, to perform the theater COMAFFOR duties and responsibilities and to work with an ad hoc crisis EUCOM JTF and component structure. Because of this, USAFE had to invest time in educating its personnel and in training the exercise personnel in the new construct and organizational processes. In moving toward the TO-BE architecture, the education and training conducted within exercises, such as AC04, will be very important. The TO-BE architecture needs personnel who are used to working in a collaborative environment in which the data owners enter the information, which is used across all the nodes. It requires systems that use machine-to-machine reporting and exhibit some automation in rolling up data into information displays for the user. The TO-BE tries to place the logistics specialist at an information vantage point from which he or she can gain knowledge over the operational environment, the commander's intent, and the ACS's potential to provide precisely defined combat capabilities. ACS education will require more training experiences like AC04 that involve the appropriate staff and C2 nodes (for example, the AOC) working together to build experience and pattern work processes. To realize the full potential of the TO-BE, a way needs to be found to involve the entire Air Force (for example, AFMC, AMC) in an exercise like AC04.[10]

Assessment team members noted that some of the challenges of AC04 related to the level of staffing normally provided in an AS-IS C2 exercise. This is primarily because of the current high operational tempo and the need to augment current staff and AOC manning. The AC04 exercise organizational structure was not fully manned and resourced. The schedule, although accelerated by the USAFE commander by one month, had three major parts that allowed a stepped process for education and training. The command clearly benefited from a December 2003 standup of the USAFE AOC (32 AOG) to 24-hour operations. This allowed permanent and augmenting personnel from the 152 AOG (New York Air National Guard) to work together prior to the exercise. The USAFE/LG also was able to conduct a base beddown exercise immediately following the initial planning conference in January 2004. In addition, the USAFE/IG tasked the USAFE staff to develop an AFEUR task list to help guide the USAFE validation of the AFEUR warfighting headquarters construct. These AC04-unique experiences helped to guide the training and fine-tune the emerging AFEUR structure and work processes. It also helped educate the entire USAFE staff and supporting organizations in baseline AOC and AFFOR duties and responsibilities.

Much of this baseline training was conducted by personnel from the Air Force Operational Command Training Program, 505th Wing, based at Hurlburt Field, Florida, as part of the former C2 Technical Integration Group. This was augmented with USAFE director of operations exercise planners and staff from the new AFEUR, USAFE/LGR, and other local

---

[10] The assessment team did include strategic partners from AFMC, AFC2ISRC, and AF/ILG in end-of-day exercise discussions. This could easily be expanded to include ACS problems for the strategic partners to work. In the AS-IS architecture, these CSC2 nodes are not generally involved in the exercise.

organizations, such as the USAFE/ U.S. Army Europe Command's WPC. Finally, USAFE is putting into place a more robust warrior training program in response to AC04 experiences and the transition to the new structure.

The AFEUR's training processes were sound and easy to follow. The USAFE commander is responsible for ensuring that training is conducted within the theater. Training covers theater challenges and knowledge and provides a foundation for global training. The AFEUR's responsibilities representing the United States as a force provider to NATO are generally covered but not in detail for this exercise because the NATO structure was outside the training audience. In the AFEUR, each AFFOR-staff functional area lead designates an individual on the staff to be responsible for monitoring and providing hands-on training for baseline assigned personnel and the AFEUR augmentees.[11] For AC04, the operational AFFOR was primarily drawn from the 16AF staff, based at Aviano AB, Italy. They were organized under an existing 16AF CONOPS that assumed the duties and responsibilities of a JTF air component staff. Each AFFOR staff carefully identified its roles and responsibilities and developed a training syllabus to document them, basing it on expected tasks, knowledge, and techniques references. As the exercise progressed through the three phases and as the structure and work relationships evolved, these documents were modified. In some cases, the documents were developed after the structure was applied in practice. The AFEUR A-9 was tasked to analyze the structure and the organization process. It is anticipated that this analysis will serve as the baseline documentation for creating new USAFE CONOPS, operational instructions, and other defining documents.

There are several ways to train personnel. They can receive one-on-one training with a trainer, complete computer-based courses on their own, or review the training documents from the Web site. Once the training is complete, the trainees must pass written and practical tests that objectively measure their individual levels of knowledge and guarantees they are qualified for their wartime positions. Individual training status is documented on Air Force Form 797, with clearly defined job qualification standards.

Documentation is important. Since the AOC is being manned and operated as a weapon system, having a recognized training path for personnel assigned to the AOC is more important. This does not lessen the need for the staff to train and gain experience in a dynamic crisis operational environment, such as an exercise. Training in the staff needs to be balanced with educational opportunities that will broaden the staff member's expertise and help provide him or her a foundation of knowledge from which to act in unforeseen situations.

The TO-BE environment appears to be more flexible for getting work done. ACS professionals keep track of taskings and search for information, products, and services in novel ways. ACS-tasked staff personnel should understand what factors constrain ACS (law, directives, practice, etc.). This will enable the COMAFFOR staff to reduce the effects of such factors or eliminate them completely when external factors change. Success here is usually a factor of a

---

[11] The AFEUR is configured as a staff with a C2 capability similar to that of a CAT. A staff is generally not manned for 24-hour operations. Augmentation is therefore necessary to be able to provide the AOC and operational JTF component AFFOR staff with information, products, and services. The augmentation was created for the exercise from the USAFE staff, USAFE NAFs, and available unit manpower, with some reserve participation through volunteers.

broad understanding of ACS structure, functional expertise, and local knowledge. Staff training to foster this level of understanding was apparent to assessment team members during AC04. ACS personnel clearly had mentally worked through different support and force beddown factors.[12] In moving to the TO-BE, the staff, at all levels, needs appropriate training programs (tabletop exercises, COA analysis, etc.) to help shape wartime roles in working with the AOC and leveraging the Air Force ACS supporting capability.

Since the AFEUR was a new organization during the exercise, its staff created and evolved its CONOPS during the three phases of the exercise. Its role as the theater warfighter staff is still evolving. The experience provided an educational opportunity to gain knowledge about the duties, responsibilities, and authorities of an organization fulfilling a new niche. Working within the AC04 context helped it define and operationalize its working CONOPS. The new organizational construct and the ad hoc exercise scenario created a steep learning curve. When fully functioning, the AFFOR will provide key information to all ACS nodes about how ACS should configure itself to support the warfighter.

Passing on a thorough understanding of the new organizational structure and the roles and responsibilities not just of the participant's organization but of each organization in the training audience was an important aspect of the training. Training focused primarily on the supporting systems and infrastructure to be used in the exercise. The two AFFOR staffs had a better knowledge base to build on because the current AS-IS systems were primarily personal computer–based and configured to support staff work. For AC04, education was generally the critical element. This enabled participants to work through systems issues and exercise-induced problems with data flows.

In the AC04 organizations that did not have a firm understanding of their roles in the greater warfighting enterprise, there was a tendency to revert back to manual processes and legacy AS-IS functional approaches to accomplish warfighter ACS tasks. This was observed early in Phase II, when the AFEUR was just beginning to function and work. Approaches were stovepiped rather than coordinated across nodes with the operational AFFOR and AOC (as suggested in the Falconer AOC's *Flight Manual* and JFACC handbook). Another example is the AOC logistics team, which gained confidence in its ability as it reached out to the operational AFFOR staff to solve problems beyond its own abilities. In both cases, the greater awareness that comes from education, understanding concepts and processes, affected outcomes more than training in hardware or software systems did.

Implications
The COMAFFOR is the leader in helping to define how ACS will meet warfighter requirements. ACS TO-BE education and training need to be sensitive to this fact in peacetime, as well as in the more-imperative wartime situation. The USAFE staff is working to perfect processes and training in an effort to move toward the CSC2 TO-BE operational architecture. Systems training is important, but it must be conducted within the context of a unit mission and role. Likewise, Air Force ACS training needs a venue in which to build experience across

---

[12] The USAFE staff certainly gained some of this understanding during Operation Iraqi Freedom, during which force beddown was shifted among EUCOM AOR bases because of host-nation constraints.

the CSC2 nodes. Role-players will not have the dynamic capability to respond as exercise play gets under way and will not have the mission fidelity to function fully within a TO-BE collaborative workspace. Better understanding of the need for a robust and assertive IM plan should be an educational goal for AFFOR and AOC educational programs. An early investment in education will help define the work process, systems, and infrastructure requirements for ACS-tasked personnel. Increased emphasis on obtaining and using collaborative tools would increase efficiencies and effectiveness until future network-centric solutions are developed.

Education and training affect culture and the approach to work. The institution of the Air Force holds overall responsibility for ensuring that personnel understand and will operationalize ACS in their daily work. The Air Force should ensure that ACS functions and processes have sufficient personnel and systems. ACS must follow the COMAFFOR's lead in establishing how ACS connects with and supports the JFC's warfighter support. The primary means the JFC and the affected COMAFFOR have for adapting forces for their specific warfighting tasks is in theater training and in exercises like AC04. Thus, it important that all Air Force ACS elements participate in exercises like AC04.

ACS education starts early. The TO-BE strategy requires ACS-aware personnel to be deliberate in their demands for systems and work processes that help them focus on and anticipate the warfighter need. This is possible only if they are prepared and have access to a TO-BE–like environment.

Summary of Recommendations

Today, the Air Force finds itself deployed globally, often on short notice, and with resources stretched to the breaking point. Movement toward the CSC2 TO-BE operational architecture will help improve C2 through better systems, tools, machine-to-machine data exchange, and a standardized organizational structure that all ACS personnel are familiar with. The TO-BE will also help facilitate ACS collaborative work groups that will help leverage the deep ACS expertise, wherever it is across the Air Force. If done correctly, this will allow sharing and work collaboration without confusing command authority or responsibility for specific tasks.[13] These improvements in C2 will enhance the ability of Air Force ACS to provide ACS to the combatant commander.

The assessment team used AC04 to generate combat support issues that crossed CSC2 nodes within the AC04 exercise's JOA and for the theater that supported the forward JTF. The USAFE exercise provided the operational environment in which the assessment team identified a range of issues affecting the move to a notional TO-BE ACS operational architecture. These issues included organization, leadership, personnel, doctrine, and training.

Following is a summary of the specific recommendations the assessment team made in response to its observations during AC04 and its knowledge of the TO-BE operational architecture.

---

[13] To a degree, this is already being done in other functional areas, such as ISR.

Organizational Structure

Clearly define command relationships including roles and responsibilities:

- between nodes (operational AFFOR to theater AFFOR and operational AFFOR to AOC)
  - within nodes (AFFOR staffs or with AOC divisions or teams)
  - within virtual collaborative workspaces
- across the entire Air Force ACS community providing combat support.

Integrate combat support planning with the operational campaign planning process:

- better integration of AFFOR capabilities and processes into the AOC to
  - facilitate specific work tasks
  - facilitate broad sharing of information
- better define how ACS builds the combat capabilities and makes them available to the warfighter
- better integration of combat support personnel into AOC divisions, specifically, the Strategy and Plans Divisions to
  - allow movement away from manual data entry into areas that help add combat capability
  - aid development of decision tools that will help model alternative COAs and share information
  - leverage deep functional expertise resident in combat support organizations in CONUS.

C2 Systems Integration and Decision-Support Tools

Establish a common system architecture for all nodes that will

- incorporate efficient and effective tools, including collaborative tools that accommodate joint, combined, and commercial systems requirements and present information gained across CSC2 nodes
- adapt and use these for peacetime management to allow wartime and peacetime CSC2 systems to merge
- promote ACS professional analysis capability at each level.

Standardize data reporting criteria and work practices across nodes (data quality, assurance, and format) to

- enable users to import shared data into forms and formats, as needed
- allow dynamic reporting with drill-down capability
- enable visibility of the IWS structure within the context of its use
- create an IM strategy across Air Force ACS.

Training and Education

Initiate CSC2 training, either as part of existing courses or as a standalone course, as required:

- train together as an enterprise within a realistic operational environment (for example, AC04)
- look for opportunities to leverage and train specialized expertise not resident in theater.

Peacetime training should mirror contingency demands and wartime operations:

- must work within the specific joint force warfighting environment
- peacetime COMAFFOR role and infrastructure (AOC and AFFOR staff) must provide a foundation for meeting JFC's need for warfighting capabilities.

Assessment Teams

Terminal Fury 2004

John Drew, RAND Corporation
Kristin Lynch, RAND Corporation
Freddie McSears, AF/ILGX
Jamie Santana, AF/ILGX
Lt Col Bruce Springs, AF/ILGC
William Williams, RAND Corporation
Lt Col Kimberlee Zorich, AF/ILGX

Austere Challenge 2004

Kristin Lynch, RAND Corporation
Freddie McSears, AF/ILGX
Jamie Santana, AF/ILGX
William Williams, RAND Corporation
Lt Col Carl Zimmerman, AFC2ISRC
Lt Col Kimberlee Zorich, AF/ILGX

Bibliography

16th AF—*See* U.S. Air Force, 16th Air Force.

502nd Air Operations Squadron—*See* U.S. Air Force, Pacific Air Forces, 502nd Air Operations Squadron.

Air Force Journal of Logistics, Vol. XXVII, No. 2, Summer 2003.

Colaizzi, Jennifer, "Extensible Mark-Up Language Exceeds Expectations During Testing," Norfolk, Va.: U.S. Joint Forces Command Public Affairs, January 20, 2005.

Dean, Keith, "Next Generation Collaboration Service/DCTS v4.0," briefing, Washington, D.C., December 2003; not available to the general public.

Deputy Chief of Staff, Air and Space Operations—*See* U.S. Air Force, Headquarters Air Force.

Falconer AOC—*See* U.S. Air Force, Falconer Air and Space Operations Center.

Isherwood, Michael, "Air Forces Europe," briefing, February 2004.

J-7 Operational Plans and Interoperability Directorate, "Joint Force Employment, Considerations Before and During Combat," briefing, undated.

———, "Logistic Support to Operations," briefing, undated.

Krisinger, Chris J., "Who We Are and What We Do: The Evolution of the Air Force's Core Competencies," *Air and Space Power Journal*, Vol. 17, No. 3, Fall 2003, pp. 15–26.

Leftwich, James A., Robert S. Tripp, Amanda Geller, Patrick H. Mills, Tom LaTourrette, Charles Robert Roll, Jr., Cauley Von Hoffman, and David Johansen, *Supporting Expeditionary Aerospace Forces: An Operational Architecture for Combat Support Execution Planning and Control*, Santa Monica, Calif.: RAND Corporation, MR-1536-AF, 2002.

Lynch, Kristin F., John G. Drew, Robert S. Tripp, and Charles Robert Roll, Jr., *Supporting Air and Space Expeditionary Forces: Lessons from Operation Iraqi Freedom*, Santa Monica, Calif.: RAND Corporation, MG-193-AF, 2005.

March, James G., *Decisions and Organizations*, Oxford, UK: Basil Blackwell Ltd., 1988.

Myers, Richard B., "A Word from the Chairman: Shift to a Global Perspective," *Air and Space Power Journal*, Vol. 17, No. 3, Fall 2003, pp. 5–10.

Office of the Secretary of Defense, *Joint Operations Concepts*, Washington, D.C., November 2003.

PACAF—*See* U.S. Air Force, Pacific Air Forces.

Tripp, Robert S., Kristin F. Lynch, John G. Drew, and Edward W. Chan, *Supporting Air and Space Expeditionary Forces: Lessons from Operation Enduring Freedom*, Santa Monica, Calif.: RAND Corporation, MR-1819-AF, 2004.

U.S. Air Force, *Organization and Employment of Aerospace Power*, Washington, D.C., Air Force Doctrine Document 2, September 28, 1998.

———, *Agile Combat Support Concept of Operations*, October 1, 1999.

———, *Base Support and Expeditionary Site Planning*, Air Force Instruction 10-404, November 26, 2001.

———, *Air and Space Commander's Handbook for the JFACC*, Air Force Doctrine Center Handbook 10-01, January 16, 2003a.

———, *Deployment Planning and Execution*, Air Force Instruction 10-403, April 14, 2003b.

———, *Command Posts*, Air Force Instruction 10-207, May 16, 2003c.

———, *United States Air Force Posture Statement*, 2004.

U.S. Air Force, Air Force Deputy Chief of Staff for Installations & Logistics, Directorate of Plans & Integration (HQ AF/ILXX) *United States Air Force Agile Combat Support Concept of Operations (USAF ACS CONOPS)*, Washington, D.C.: October 1, 1999.

U.S. Air Force, Air Force Materiel Command, *Combat Logistics Support*, AFMC Instruction 10-202, September 24, 2001.

U.S. Air Force, Air Mobility Command, *AMC Command and Control Operations*, AMC Instruction 10-207, Vol. 1, February 13, 1995.

———, *Director of Mobility Forces (DIRMOBFOR) Policy and Procedures*, AMC Instruction 10-202, Vol. 7, August 1, 2004.

U.S. Air Force, Combat Air Force, "Agile Combat Support Mission Area Plan FY2002," October 1, 2000.

U.S. Air Force, Eleventh Air Expeditionary Task Force, *Terminal Fury 2004, Exercise Operations Order* (draft), December 1, 2003.

U.S. Air Force, Falconer Air and Space Operations Center, *Flight Manual*, Vol. 1, Rev. 7, AN/USQ-163-1, November 26, 2002.

U.S. Air Force, Headquarters Air Force, Deputy Chief of Staff, Air and Space Operations, *Command and Control Concept of Operations*, July 22, 2002.

U.S. Air Force, Headquarters, Air Force, Deputy Chief of Staff, Plans and Programs, *Strategic Planning Directive for Fiscal years 2006–2023*, July 2003.

U.S. Air Force, Pacific Air Forces, *Pacific Air Mobility Operations*, PACAF Instruction 10-2101, April 13, 2001a.

———, *Command and Control Operations Procedures*, PACAF Instruction 10-601, December 7, 2001b.

———, "Joint Air and Space Operations Center Standard Operating Procedures," July 13, 2001c.

———, *PACAF Command Posts*, PACAF Instruction 10-207, October 10, 2003.

———, Operations Support Center, PACAF Exercise Terminal Fury 04 Situation Reports, December 5–9, 2003. Not available to the general public.

U.S. Air Force, Pacific Air Forces, 502nd Air Operations Squadron, *Concept of Operations for the PACAF Operations Support Center and the PACAF Contingency Action Team*, January 25, 2002.

U.S. Air Force, Sixteenth Air Force, *Sixteenth Air Force Deployed Combat Staffs Concept of Operations*, November 24, 2003.

U.S. Air Force, Thirteenth Air Force, *Air Force Forces (AFFOR) Concept of Operations*, October 7, 2003.

U.S. Air Force, Thirteenth Air Force A-6, *AFFOR C2*, briefing, October 2003.

USAFE—*See* U.S. Air Force, U.S. Air Forces in Europe.

U.S. Air Force, U.S. Air Forces in Europe, *USAFE Command Posts*, U.S. Air Forces Europe Instruction 10-207, December 31, 2003.

—— , .*Austere Challenge 04 AOC In-Flight Guide*, March 23, 2004a.

—— , *Expeditionary Site Planning Cell (A45) Concept of Operations*, draft, 2004b.

Waldrop, M. Mitchell, *Pervasive Computing: An Overview of the Concept and Exploration of the Public Policy Implications*, Washington, D.C.: Woodrow Wilson International Center for Scholars, March 2003.